That Reminds Me

THAT REMINDS ME

Stories Poems Essays Plays

for Lorelei,

Jerry Mevissen

JERRY MEVISSEN

JACKPINE WRITERS' BLOC

Send correspondence to Jackpine Writers' Bloc, Inc., 13320 149th Avenue, Menahga, Minnesota. sharrickl@wcta.net

Content Editor: Deb Schlueter
Line Editors: Sharon Harris and Marilyn Wolff
Beta Readers: Niomi Phillips and Bonnie West
Layout, Production and Cover Design: Tarah L. Wolff
Critics at Large: The Jackpine Writers' Bloc
Back cover photograph by Rich Brocaw

For Sarah, Rachel, Peter, Michael and Megan

CONTENTS

REFLECTIONS

CONTENTS

Refractions

CONTENTS

ALSO WRITTEN BY JERRY MEVISSEN

Nimrod Chronicles
Broken Hart
Good Shepherd

For more information go to:
www.JERRYMEVISSEN.com

Jackpine Writers' Bloc, Inc.
www.JACKPINEWRITERS.COM

THAT REMINDS ME

That Reminds Me

INTRODUCTION

A family gathers for Christmas dinner back at the home place, and Grandma asks a grandson about his first deer hunt. Grandpa smiles and says, "That reminds me."

Brothers gather around a campfire at the annual fishing outing on "an area lake" and reminisce about the year a rainstorm swamped the tent. A brother smiles and says, "That reminds me."

The Daughters of Martha gather for morning coffee at the senior center and discuss gardens and grandkids. A newcomer complains about a neighbor's goat in her petunia patch. A veteran wag smiles and says, "That reminds me."

For small towns in rural Minnesota, this is everyday fare. A million conversations; a million stories. It's the privilege of a storyteller to record this vanishing slice of Americana. For the past sixteen years, that's what I've done. The stories in this book are inspired by living near the small town of Nimrod, Minnesota, on a farm along the Crow Wing River. Most have been published or publicly read. This is their second debut.

The collection begins with Reflections—stories, poems, and essays in creative memoir. Never a strict historian, I don't mind bending facts if it makes a better story. It ends with Refractions, where stories are twisted and diffused to repopulate a seductive plot or re-plotted to commemorate iconic characters.

Readers may wonder why the stories never have happy endings or never end at all. Often, they just stop. That's intentional. As Arnold says in the final story of *Good Shepherd*, "There are no endings, let alone happy ones. If we're lucky, life goes on and on and on."

Enjoy.

REFLECTIONS

Creative Memoir

LOVE. BIRTH. DEATH.

W*hoever thought a moment so beautiful could last forever?*

The bride and groom picked their way down the porch steps, over the slate rock path toward the pickup truck, its antenna decorated with a crude bow of red and white crepe paper. She bunched her long dress in one hand, clutched her bouquet of garden roses in the other. The groom, thick wrists protruding beyond his sleeves, held her arm as she negotiated the uneven rock to the gravel drive. He opened the truck door and lifted her into the seat, kissed her red curls, then walked in front of the cab to the driver's side.

Two young boys, her brothers, ran behind the truck with a wire of tin cans and looped it over the rear bumper. The engine whirred, then roared, and the truck rolled forward. The mom wiped her eyes with an apron. The dad steadied himself against a porch post, then hugged his wife, pulled her close, and waved. Ribbons on gifts fluttered over the tailgate as the truck rolled away. The boys chased the truck down the driveway laughing, the dog barking, the cans rattling.

At the road, the truck turned and the bride looked back at her family, now all waving, waving, waving. She rolled the window down and managed a half-wave, then disappeared behind a grove of Chinese elm that grew along the ditch.

Whoever thought a moment so beautiful could delay itself so long?

In those days, expectant fathers waited in the delivery room lounge, paging through old *Newsweek* magazines, feigning calmness, jolting when the doors swung open and Nurse McKay called, *Mr. So-and-so, you have a baby boy.* And Mr. So-and-so, already a father, nodded his head, reached for his hat, and walked out. The rest sat, inhaling sterile hospital air, hearing an occasional muffled scream. Minutes passed, or was it hours? Days? The round clock above the swinging doors showed four, five, six o'clock. AM or PM?

THAT REMINDS ME

Why don't you go to the cafeteria? Nurse McKay said. *It will be a while.*

Down the hall, down the stairs, past the cafeteria to the front door, he stood on the hospital entry and inhaled, exhaled, inhaled, exhaled. A light snow fell. Headlights and taillights indicated rush hour traffic. Morning or night? Why is her labor protracted? Will she be all right? Will the baby survive?

Back in the waiting room, Nurse McKay said, *You may come in for a few minutes.*

She lay on her back, knees bent, and forced a smile. Her skin was damp, her red hair wet. He dabbed her with a towel, her forehead, her cheeks, her neck, her chest. She squeezed his hand with unexpected force, then placed it on her distended belly. *Soon,* she mouthed. *Soon.* Nurse McKay motioned for him to leave.

A muffled scream, another, another. He squeezed his eyes shut, gripped the arm rests, felt bile rise in his throat. Minutes passed. Quiet. The expectant fathers eyed each other. *Yours? Mine?* The red second hand on the wall clock swept around and around and around.

Nurse McKay opened the door, walked to him, and smiled. *You have a baby boy.*

He reached for her, attempted to stand, wobbled. Tears flooded his eyes and streamed down his cheeks. Tried to say, *Thank you* or something, anything. Nothing. *You can see her in her room in a few minutes,* she said.

Down the hall, down the stairs to the chapel, he knelt before the altar of the Blessed Virgin, buried his head in his working-man hands, and trembled.

At the altar's bouquet, he traced his finger around a rose, then walked out to the hospital entry. Snowflakes swirled and levitated. Floating to the sidewalk, he hovered over pure, fresh snow and glided forward. He thought of calling her mom and dad on the farm. Somewhere a carillon bell rang. He looked down at his side, extended a gloveless finger, and felt his son's tiny grip.

Whoever thought a moment of sorrow could be a moment of joy?

After her funeral, he led the procession with a team of mottled Percherons that bore her coffin on a caisson down Main Street from First Lutheran to the graveyard. The church bell tolled, tolled, tolled seventy-nine times, one for each year of her life. When the *dust thou art* was dusted, the compulsory well wishes wished, the customary sandwiches consumed, he returned to the home place where they farmed and aged together. Her flower garden was overgrown and unkempt, the kitchen chilled and vacant, the bed lonely and depressing.

He moved to a small stuccoed bungalow with blue shutters on Main Street and built a garden in the front yard—roses and bridal wreath that reminded him of her. The following year, he extended the garden to the side yard with mock orange and clematis, to the other side with tulips and daffodils, day lilies and forsythia. The backyard remained intact, shaded by an orchard of apples and plums.

He attended the flowers with the love he attended her—careful soil preparation, timely food and water, constant cultivation. The garden responded, and flowers bloomed in primary colors and pastels —zinnias pink to red, marigolds yellow to orange, delphinium white to blue; in a variety of heights—crawling ground phlox to six-foot hollyhocks: in a jungle of shapes—spires of violet larkspur to mounds of copper asters.

Garden clubs drove from neighboring towns. The school art class sketched and painted the blooms. A reporter from the county newspaper photographed him in the garden and ran a story.

Flowers proliferated. He carried bouquets to the church on Sunday, the nursing home daily, the senior center on lunch days. The clinic waiting room, the post office lobby, the tellers at the bank, the teachers at school, all received bouquets. Townspeople notified him of baptisms, birthdays, and anniversaries. They received bouquets. He delivered armloads of flowers, rose phlox bouncing off his shoulders, white daisies tickling his chin.

The summer passed, the garden flourished. His clientele grew, and in early September, when roses peaked and chrysanthemum burst into bloom and golden marigolds challenged the sun, he died.

The funeral service was brief, the attendance sparse. After the pallbearers lifted the casket onto the caisson, the church bell tolled, tolled, tolled eighty-four times. The team of Percherons clomped down Main Street leading the cortege toward the graveyard.

It passed the senior center and diners, waiting and holding flowers, joined the procession. Passed the school where students stood in the parking lot, each with flowers. Passed Erickson Grocery where clerks flipped the *Open* sign, each holding flowers, and joined the procession. Passed the nursing home where residents waited in wheelchairs and on walkers, their caretakers steadying them, all carrying flowers. The bank, the post office, the feed mill, the hardware store, the clinic. Down Main Street, an undulating ribbon of colors— red and white and yellow and crimson and orange and violet and blue and pink and green and rose and coral and lavender . . .

BLUE MASON JAR

Hot coffee streams along the knife
and keeps the jar from breaking
She towels warm baked bread
and packs it in a pail

In the field, man pitches hay onto a wagon
Atop, boy pulls the hay and stomps
Horses sweat, reins slung across their backs
Man lifts his hat and wipes his dusty brow

He sees her cross the field and motions to boy
She pours coffee lukewarm in stoneware mugs
sepia brown the way the man drinks it
rich with cream and sugar

They talk and boy feeds flicks of clover to the team
Man sweeps his arm across the windrows
drains his cup and swings it in an arc
She packs the jar and cups and walks

Years later boy/man tastes sweet coffee
and smells whiffs of fresh mowed hay
Coffee warm and rich the way he drank it
poured from a blue Mason jar

THAT REMINDS ME

COFFEE

Isn't it you who's stimulated by aromas? Digging the garden in spring and smelling warm earth? Walking through fresh cut hay? At a summer barbecue, first catching the smell of burning charcoal and then . . . New York strips. I know how you feel. Coffee does that to me.

Listen to it percolate, its five-note arpeggio like a Philip Glass composition. Inhale that aroma. The beachside walkup at Carmel comes to mind. The adobe Starbucks in Santa Fe. Coffee: comfort. Comfort: coffee. Made for each other, like *Funk & Wagnalls.*

I pour a mug and motion to you. No, you'll decline. You'll have water. Not bottled: tap. That's the kind of creature you are. No pretensions. No airs and graces. Yours is the new green sophistication.

I stir in a heaping tablespoon of Cool Whip, one of my indulgences. Doesn't that look good? And the taste. It speaks to you, but doesn't sass.

You wait.

It's late November. I sit on a wicker sofa in the sunroom. Morning light floods the room, blinding me. You don't sit beside me. You sit on a pillowed chair opposite, as if there'll be discussion, perhaps a decision this morning. I stir my coffee and feel the spoon's pattern on my thumb. I look at the spoon. New York World's Fair, 1964. Where did that come from? I'm stalling.

"Coffee is a paradox," I say, more to myself than to you. "Both stimulant and relaxant. Like insulation. Keeps you warm and keeps you cool." I'm biding time. You don't respond. The sun shines on your shoulders and gleams through your auburn hair. Gives you an angelic aura, one that insists that, regardless how long I procrastinate, you'll have your way.

I hold the mug in both hands and feel its warmth. I sip, swallow, and sigh. "Ah, the nectar of the mortals."

You're impatient. You shift in your chair and raise your eyes to mine, demanding and non-negotiable.

Your impatience weighs on me. Yes, you deserve my response. But can't it wait? Must it be now? This moment? Now, when coffee is saving my life?

You don't relent.

"Ambrosia," I say. I lift the mug and drain the last drops. I'm emboldened by the caffeine. "All right," I sigh, and rise.

You sense my capitulation, jump from the chair, and rush to me.

I look at you and offer my hand. "Rover, would you like to walk?"

BRIDGES

I'm uneasy standing in front of my boyhood home in south Minneapolis. Guilty, shamed, tormented. I remember our house as small and nondescript, and it is. All the houses are small, aligned in dreary repetition like Monopoly pieces, gray and dilapidated. The lilac bush we planted shades the front yard. Irises grow at random beside the stoop. A patch of green, maybe mint descended from my mother's herb garden, follows the picket fence that separates our house from the neighbors.

Shame and sadness overwhelm me, force me to leave. I drive to Riverside Park, past the Metro Theater that showed war movies— *Guadalcanal Diary* and *Sands of Iwo Jima*. Past the Fire Station where white-helmeted Civil Defense wardens gathered to patrol the neighborhood on brown-out nights. Past the public school where gates to the playground are locked, on to the Franklin Avenue bridge. I walked this route many times with my friend Freddie Lambin, his sister Donna, his little brother Danny who, at six years old, had lost his right arm to a wringer wash machine. Danny followed Freddie like a dog. I remember our slow and easy summers.

"What now?" Freddie asked when we saw the sign at Riverside Park pool that read *Closed Until Further Notice.* "Must be the polio epidemic."

We agreed to walk to the Franklin Avenue bridge over the Mississippi. The beach there was modest, an outcropping of littered rock and a lean shelf of gravel that stretched into the river. The shoreline current was slow in August, and, if it got the better of us, we swam towards a concrete strut, caught our breath, and scrambled to shore. I was the oldest kid, the best swimmer.

Freddie warned Danny to stay on the narrow shelf of gravel that dropped off into the river channel. Danny contented himself with tossing driftwood sticks upstream and retrieving them as they floated by. He must have lost his balance.

We heard him scream, saw his stub arm flail. Freddie swam for him, then turned to shore when Danny floated farther into the current. I took a deep breath and swam toward him, surfacing to spot him, then swimming again. Swimming, surfacing, buoyed by panic. Swimming, surfacing. Feeling unreal, like a dream, like everything would be okay when I woke.

When I last surfaced, the river was dark and gentle, with soft eyes of white foam.

We knew of the Riverside Fire Station within a block of the bridge. "I'll run for help," I screamed. "You guys stay here."

I didn't wait to ride in the squad car back to the bridge. I ran back and beat the truck by seconds. Freddie paced up and down the rocky shore yelling for Danny. Donna sat on a rock, waving her arms and sobbing, "No, no, no."

The firemen scrambled down the bank in yellow hip boots and black jackets. They dragged coils of ropes and life preservers and nets. "Stay on shore," they yelled. "Get back up on the bridge."

We huddled on the sidewalk, confused and shivering. Donna wrapped her arms around her body and wailed. When a crowd gathered beside the firetruck, we turned our backs to them and watched the confusion below.

In time, the rescue squad climbed the bank, restored their equipment, and drove away. The chief offered us a ride home in his red car. A metal grid separated the front seat from the back. Doors were handle-less. The radio cracked with emergency transmissions. The seats were hard, hot leather.

The police questioned us at the Lambin house later that afternoon, Mrs. Lambin hysterical, Freddie scared, Mr. Lambin furious. He glared at me and interrupted the questioning. "What were you doing in the river? Didn't you know it was dangerous? Who watched Danny?"

The police left, and my mother returned home. I sat with Freddie in his room, his and Danny's room, with Danny's shirt flung across the bed, the right arm sewed shut. Neither of us spoke. Mr. Lambin climbed the stairs, heavy-footed and enraged. He grabbed my shoulders and shook me.

"Danny drowned," he screamed. "How do you like them

apples?" He shook me again until I bounced off his body. "What's the matter with you? I thought you were the hot shot swimmer. Couldn't save a fifty-pound kid?"

He pushed me away. I crumbled to the floor, wriggling to avoid his boots.

"Weakling," he screamed. "Sissy, weakling."

I drive to the bridge now, thirty years later, a daily swimmer, representing my health club in competitions. The area below the bridge is fenced and posted. *No Trespassing. Danger, Keep Out. No Swimming.* I scale the fence and jump to the ground. It's August, hot and humid, the kind of day that tempts a swimmer. I strip to my briefs and wade in. The water is cool, refreshing. I step off the gravel ledge into the current and dive under. Thirty feet from shore, I surface and let the current carry me toward the bridge strut. A branch is anchored there, snagging driftwood, a plastic bottle, fragments of foam insulation.

I toss the largest piece of driftwood into the current, give it a few seconds, take a deep breath, and swim after it. My breathing is efficient; my strokes are strong. The driftwood bobs in and out of sight, floating with casual ease with the current. The chopped water surface reduces my strokes to thrashes. The driftwood disappears. One last attempt. One final scan. Nothing.

I lie on the shore drying on the rock outcropping. Above, I hear the peaceful hum of traffic, the downshift of a semi, the roar of a plane lifting from Minneapolis-St. Paul International. Flies buzz around the abandoned skeleton of a fish. Foxtail grass, faded to tan, waves from a fissure in the rock.

A faint breeze rises from the river. A light breeze, innocent and redeeming.

SINGLE SPACE

This morning, I rise from bed, roused by a feeling of complete rest and an urge to enjoy the day. I turn the radio on to my favorite station, make a pot of coffee to the stoutness I desire, and slip into yesterday's jeans that would pass muster only for a bachelor.

I step outside with my first cup of coffee, slide into a pair of mud-laden boots, and walk the dog to the corral to count cattle and horses and greet them by name. I scratch Ben, the Percheron gelding, and Coral and Shadow and Crystal. In time, I return to the house for a second cup of coffee and, in more time, breakfast. No schedule, no accommodating another's schedule, no complaints about smelling like a horse. Such is single life.

Insurance actuaries contend that married men live longer than single men, and maybe they do. But stress is known to shorten life. My stress, if any, is self-induced. I go to bed when I'm tired, and eat when I'm hungry. No longer do I wait to use the bathroom, tolerate banal television dialog while I read, or ask permission to go to the local bar & grill for happy hour. And the toothpaste tube is always squeezed from the bottom.

Having said that, there are times when I miss a spouse's sharing presence. A dramatic sunset. Dancing northern lights. Baltimore orioles at the feeder. I'm uncomfortable sitting in a movie theater alone. And it would be gratifying to see a light in the window when I return at night, or smell the aroma of pot roast or chocolate chip cookies when I walk in the door.

Married friends come to visit and we talk common interests for a while. Then *she* says, "You should have someone to share your home, share your life." She talks about a widowed friend who leads an active, interesting life—loves to travel, is financially independent, takes care of herself. We set up a dinner date at my home for the four of us. Over a 2004 Robert Hall Cabernet Sauvignon, a good brie, and sliced Pink

Lady apples, we chat before the fireplace. She offers an account of a shopping trip to the new Walmart with her granddaughter; I offer an account of a canoe expedition with my grandson to the Boundary Waters. She talks of her 500 card club; I talk of my new orchard project and halter-breaking new colts. She chuckles about getting on a bicycle and riding around the block without falling. I counter with an account of risking a black diamond ski run at Copper Mountain.

Time for dinner, and I pull out all the stops. Candlelight. Fresh flowers. A Dave Brubeck CD. On the menu, mesclun lettuce salad with orange slices, almonds, and a raspberry vinaigrette. Seafood fettuccini with a recipe reconstructed from a San Diego bistro. Garlic buttered bread sticks. And homemade cranberry sorbet for dessert. She eyes the dinner table set to Emily Post standards, the presentation of the entrée, and whispers to her friend, "I'll never have this guy over for dinner."

Mission accomplished. Funny that the husbands never volunteer that *they* know a widowed lady friend.

Contemporary American society favors marriage. As does the ultimate arbiter, the New Testament, which says it's not good for man to be alone, and Adam lost a rib because of it. Vacation rates are priced per couple. Restaurant tables are set for two. A single man, arriving alone, is viewed with indifference or suspicion.

Living alone engenders feelings of independence, of responsibility to and for myself. I'm cautious because there's no one there to miss me if I don't return. My independence is reflected in my home which represents me, and me alone. Comfortable furniture. Un-curtained windows. Morning coffee cups stacked in the sink. Scattered piles of reading and writing material.

I see an older couple driving down Highway 10 and fantasize they are married and traveling to visit grandchildren. They talk to each other, grin and laugh. She watches him; he sneaks a peek at her while driving. Fifty years of marriage and they're still in love. What an accomplishment. What a coincidence. Two people were attracted to each other years ago, grew old together, obviously took separate paths but stayed on the same road. I envy them.

But not for me. I invite friends and neighbors to share a bowl of soup on a last minute whim, regardless of how clean the house is, how manicured the lawn is, how badly I need a shave. They come and go. I come and go, unattached. Alone, but not lonely.

STATE OF THE UNION

Thank you all, Mr. Speaker, Vice President Cheney, members of Congress, members of the Supreme Court and diplomatic corps, distinguished guests, and fellow citizens. Tonight, the state of the union is strong—and together we will make it stronger. (Applause.)

It was President Bush's second State of the Union address. I was one of the 400 distinguished guests in the Capitol chambers gallery, courtesy of a pass from Congressman Jim Oberstar. I considered the offer before accepting, having been a critic of this administration, short on domestic and foreign policy and long on partisan showmanship. I didn't want to be a part of the political pep fest. Vaudeville without the baggy pants.

The flip side of the argument was the opportunity to be present in the same hallowed hall of the U.S. Capitol with the President, Vice President, the Senate, House of Representatives, Cabinet, Supreme Court justices, and diplomatic corps. The historical perspectives prevailed. I accepted the invitation.

Every step toward freedom makes our country safer. So we will act boldly in freedom's cause. (Applause.)

On the night of January 31, 2006, the Capitol District was under a state of siege. After days of unseasonable warmth (cherry blossoms were reported earlier in the day), a cold north wind blew in. Streets around the Capitol were barricaded. Sidewalks were cordoned off with green rubberized chain link fence. Every stripe of law enforcement—D.C. police, U.S. Capitol police, FEMA emergency response teams, Federal troopers, and secret service agents—patrolled every intersection. It turned cold, and I had opted to walk, coatless, from the hotel for what was certain to be less time-consuming than the circuitous cab ride. Red and blue lights flashed with strobe-like precision. Guy wires clacked against tall, metal flag poles. Sirens wailed down Pennsylvania Avenue. A helicopter circled the Capitol dome.

Every step makes our country safer. (Applause.)

I have never seen my country so defended, so paranoid, so insecure.

But our enemies and friends can be certain. The United States will not retreat from the world, and we will never surrender to evil. (Applause.)

This far into the speech, the scripting was obvious. An emotional chestnut (*Never surrender to evil*); a call to patriotism (*We are in this fight to win, and we are winning.*); a bit of Yankee jingoism (*Together, let us . . . lead the world toward freedom.*) All elicited standing ovations. Republican congress members sat on the right, Democrats on the left. In time, the left side remained seated. Their applause was lame to non-existent. The right side remained energized and sprang to its collective feet on cue. I was surprised by the uniformity of dress. Republicans wore red ties; Democrats wore blue. The President wore a neutral black and blue check. First Lady Laura Bush wore a bi-partisan pink.

One bit of upstaged drama. Anti-war activist Cindy Sheehan sat in the gallery about ten seats away. She removed her jacket to expose a T-shirt with the message *How Many More?* Secret Service agents descended en masse and escorted her quietly and efficiently out of the gallery. I read later she had been warned that such displays were not allowed in the Capitol chambers. She was arrested and charged with unlawful conduct.

The administration promoted the speech as being strong on domestic policy, light on foreign. But the first half was foreign policy. And much of it was not new. The President made one surprising reference to *weapons of mass destruction*, which I expected to be anathema to the Administration by now. Fortunately, he didn't repeat an earlier mantra—*stay the course.*

Once into domestic policy, the President piqued my attention with his Advanced Energy Initiative, a 22% increase in clean energy research including *"zero-emission coal-fired power plants, revolutionary solar and wind technologies, and clean, safe nuclear power."* (Applause.)

This program supported my reason for being in Washington— to provide grass roots support for political issues that face Todd-Wadena Electric Co-op. Fourteen Minnesota Co-op board members met all eight Minnesota congressmen/women and two senators to discuss pending legislation and promote our accomplishments.

Pending legislation included relief from excessive rail rates for captive shippers, return to market rates for preference power, and imposition of reasonable reductions in CO_2 emissions. Accomplishments included development of coal-drying technology, an international project to electrify a small Haitian village, and use of USDA's Rural Development Loan and Grant program where we created 2,200 jobs in Minnesota Co-op territory.

The second announcement that roused me was the American Competitiveness Initiative *"to encourage innovation throughout our economy, and to give our nation's children a firm grounding in math and science."* (Applause.)

Although the pronouncement lacked the drama and sweep of President John F. Kennedy's Man-to-the-Moon initiative, it received a warm reception. (One week later, the President released his budget showing funds for education reduced.)

About an hour later, (thirty minutes of speech and thirty minutes of applause), the show was over. Members of Congress hugged and kissed and shook hands—on their side of the aisle. "A love feast," said Lisa, a South Carolina staffer on my right. "Everybody loves everybody." Well, not quite.

I scanned the floor below for familiar faces. Vice President Dick Cheney, Secretary of State Condoleezza Rice, Attorney General Alberto Gonzales, Secretary of Defense Donald Rumsfeld. Judges Alito, Thomas, and Roberts. Senators Orrin Hatch, Mitch McConnell, newly elected Minnesotan Amy Klobuchar, and Hillary Clinton who was smaller and created less buzz than I expected. Said Congressman Colin Peterson the next day, "Out of town, she's a rock star. Here she's just another senator."

One aspect of the speech I missed was the television camera's intrusive panning the audience—the grimace, the pencil tap, the thunderous applause and the four-finger clap. That and the opposition's rebuttal. Small price to pay, however, to see history made, to sit in chambers with the most powerful people on the planet, to register my approval or disapproval with impunity.

The walk back to the hotel replayed the walk to the Capitol. Agents shepherded us out a side door where two limousines waited. The smaller of the two sported a door seal of *Vice President of the United States*. We scurried. Squadrons of motorcycles waited on Capitol Circle.

U.S. Capitol police rushed us through an intersection. Guards, some with dogs, patrolled the streets. The motorcade left the Capitol, preceded by police cars, motorcycle guards, emergency rescue vehicles, then two limousines hidden between speeding armed cars and more motorcycle guards. Red and blue lights flashed. Sirens wailed.

The chill north wind restored me to reality. Distant sirens. Fading flashing lights. Street guards moving slowly or standing quietly as if in a dream. A kettle-pounding protest group chanted "Bush back down. People rise up." Flags billowed. The helicopter circled the illuminated Capitol dome, bright and beautiful, dominating the night sky.

As President Bush said in his closing words, "May God bless America." (Applause, applause, applause.)

MY MEMOIR BOOTS

Born and bred for lace-up boots
Parcel post from Sears and Roebuck

Dairy farming in Wisconsin
Milking Holsteins after school

Drafted in the U.S. Army
Forward march in basic training

Student, husband, father, mayor
Hobby farms in western suburbs

Camping in the Rocky Mountains
Climbing Eagle Peak at dawn

Honeywell for three long decades
Planning, waiting to retire

Fun vacations with the grandkids
Bound'ry Waters trip with Peter

Ski train to Whitefish Montana
Michael samples mountain boarding

Hiking, touring Costa Rica
Lava flows at La Fortuna

Home on Crow Wing, riding horses
Big Ben drops me for a loss

Now still booted, chores and writing
Working on my legacy

THAT REMINDS ME

OUT TO PASTURE

Gus is tentative as he walks to the trailer. His handler is gentle, easy paced. He reassures Gus, says "Good boy. Good bye," and strokes his neck. The trailer is new to Gus, but he has loaded before. The step into the trailer presents a challenge. In earlier years, he would have jumped. Today he stops, measures the rise, and twists his body, raising one leg, then another.

Gus is a Haflinger stallion, retiring after twenty-odd years. His knees are swollen from arthritis, his legs are bowed, his hips sunken. He walks like an old man, shoulders protruding and head bobbing with each step. The trailer transports him to Brigadoon Farm, his and my final stop. Steve the veterinarian watches Gus lumber out of the trailer, purses his lips, and says there's nothing to be done. "I can't cure him. All you can do is keep him comfortable. Give him plenty of pasture. Expect to find him lying down, resting a lot."

Gus fulfills my plan to breed Haflinger horses, a small draft breed that originated in Austria. Renowned for their gentle spirit and easy keeping, they are both draft and riding horses, perfect companions for growing old.

Mocha the Haflinger mare is tethered to a fence post in the corral to avoid a confrontation with Gus at the gate. She watches him unload from the trailer. Gus stops when he sees her, raises his head in a calendar pose, and whinnies. He leads like a gentleman to the gate, but all that changes with the click of the lead rope latch. He's a young stallion again. Proud. Aggressive. Virile. Spirit burns in his eyes. His nostrils flare. His coat shines like burnished bronze. In an instant, he establishes the equine pecking order at Brigadoon. Gus is King Gustav.

He's not satisfied with his legacy, his progeny of tens, scores, maybe hundreds of foals. He has found inspiration and opportunity at Brigadoon to reproduce and increase his legacy. To live, then die, in dignity.

THAT REMINDS ME

And so it is. At some point, if good fortune deems, we reach our destination where body, mind, and spirit unite. Home. Brigadoon. There are challenges—livestock to tend, buildings to maintain, lawn to mow, gardens to cultivate, firewood to split and stack, machinery to maintain. But with the challenges, rewards—fulfillment of the need to nurture someone, something during the empty nest phase; gratification from satisfying the herd's need for food, water, and shelter; the company of friends and neighbors sharing a cup of coffee; and the opposite—solitude, surrounded by quaking aspens, warbling wrens, the calming river current, the stillness of Sophia lying at my feet.

This is inspiration for production, if not of progeny then of prose. Local lore narrated in colorful idioms beckons to be recorded. Events and characters, enriched by repeated telling, are the stuff of fiction.

Gus hobbles with Mocha to the stable. Mocha joins him. He has found home. As long as he is able, he will graze the pasture with his stable mates.

He is alive. Old, yes, but alive.

SAWYER

His hands
blue veins bulge from knuckles
to a gray-haired wrist where he wears a watch.
But why? He measures time in hours until dark.

His other wrist
a tarnished copper band.
Keeps the rheumatism down, he says.
At sixty-nine, you gotta play the angles.

His shirt
buttoned at the neck and cuffs
despite the sweat of late July.
Gray ribbing peeks at neck and sleeves.

His jeans
faded, worn, and patched.
His seamstress fancies sewing not an art.
Stitches ramble. Sometimes fabrics match.

His stature
abbreviated
bent from bending.
A willow whipped by wind.

His saw
maintained better than his truck
or health or house or home.
Gleaming chain teeth gnaw at giants.

He tugs the starter cord. The saw bucks
and screams until the trigger lock's released.
He sets the choke and thumps the oiler knob.

He scans the oak before the felling cut
and points the saw.
I'll fell it to my left, right on that stump.

The man
drops the tree on target.
He tilts the visored cap with blue-veined hand
then grins and wipes the sweat, the dust.

MINOR EVENT: MAJOR MIRACLE

Today, the last Sunday of January, one hundred and thirty million people watch the Super Bowl. I have the world to myself. I start the tractor and haul hay bales for the livestock. It's pleasant for a late January afternoon, low twenties with the sun hovering above the trees across the river. There's slight snow, four or five inches, enough to cover the barnyard but not enough to warrant chains for the tractor.

The twelve head of Scottish Highland cattle feed close to the barn. With warm temperatures, they eat less, and hay spills around the feeders. Not wasted, but used as bedding for afternoon naps.

After feeding, I lean against the gate and observe. The cattle reciprocate; they stop eating and watch me. Kelly the collie doesn't know what to make of quiet time. She sits. The cattle are content—well-fed, clear eyes, straight backs, dense coats of copper hair. And impressive racks of mottled gray horns. Six of the cows are pregnant, with one delivery imminent.

MacDuff, the patriarch, is magnificent with his 36-inch horn span, his thick muscled neck and wavy amber hair, his extended torso that moves like an articulated bus.

Three calves, born in spring, are tame now. They follow me into the barn at the sight of the grain bucket and save themselves the trouble of battling for space at the feed trough.

With six pregnant cows, I feed a molasses supplement. The expectant mothers wear molasses masks around their mouths.

One cow, the imminent delivery one, strays from the herd into the woods. Her signs have been evident for weeks. Swollen belly, depression behind the hipbones, vaginal secretion. I've done the math; the cows began calving in early spring last year. If MacDuff did his job, and he is conscientious, the cows were bred in May. Nine months later is February, and today is January 30.

The pregnant cow waddles into the woods of the south pasture a few steps at a time. She evaluates the area as a delivery site, then disappears deeper into the woods. I walk along the fence, watching her. She watches me. Kelly walks by my side, with an instinct greater than mine for impending birth.

I note my location—a white oak stump remaining from a tree that fell across the fence in last summer's wind storm. The snow in the woods is marked with deer tracks and an occasional rabbit or squirrel trail, but the cow's hoof prints are easily discernible. I leave her there, standing in the woods. Her instincts have told her to leave the safety of the herd to deliver her calf. Does she know that a mild night is predicted? Does she know that coyotes howl at the north end of the pasture?

Back at the barn, the temperature is still twenty degrees, and I head for the house. It's five-thirty. I carry split jack pine from the woodpile and feed the fireplace where logs burn easily and hot with a rich pine aroma. I wonder about the cow. But the fire is warm, the flames dance hypnotically, and the couch is inviting. I succumb. Kirby, the house dog, finds a comfortable spot in the crook of my knees, and we nap.

Supper is light, shared with a magazine for distraction. I read that an inch of humus represents 1,000 years of time.

At 8:30, I finish the magazine and dress for a walk to the woods with a flashlight. As I step outside, I feel tolerable night air. No wind, and a temperature of sixteen degrees. The moon is behind a cloud bank. Stars shine. The sky is black velvet; stars are slightly beyond reach. The Milky Way dominates the sky, north to south. I check the Big Dipper to confirm that we agree on which direction is north.

Kelly walks beside me as we cross the gate into the barnyard. I count the cows at the bale feeder before we trek into the woods. Nine lying down, two feeding, one missing. I count again and shine the light to the barn. Nothing there. Still missing one. I count a third time. Eleven.

Kelly and I head for the oak stump to pick up the trail. It leads randomly east, then south, east, then south through thickets and over deadfalls. The cow's hoof prints are easy to track, fresh and large compared to deer tracks crisscrossing them. I spot a small circle around a tree where she had rested in an area of hoof-packed snow, then left. The trail leads westerly now, toward the only rise in the pasture. It proceeds toward a clearing at the top of the rise, ten feet away from a deer stand.

I call the cow, knowing that I am within hearing distance, not wanting to startle her. Or them. I stop and shine the light in an arc on the trail. Nothing. I come to a large oak, and beneath it the snow is trampled. Not the right site. Kelly and I continue. Another large oak and another trampled site. Kelly stays close. I shine the light and pick up two glossy reflections between a set of horns. The cow is facing me, about twenty-five feet distant. I lower the light to the ground and spot two more glossy reflections. Smaller, but as bright.

It's total peace. Nothing moves. Nothing sounds. "Silent Night" comes to mind. I talk to the new mother in soft, encouraging words. "Such a fine baby. Such a good mother."

Baby lies beside mother under a Norway pine in an area of trampled snow, on 1,000 years of humus. Mother is licking him, or her, cleaning the residue of birth and stimulating young muscles to stand and make the vital steps to its first feeding. Mother is impervious to me now and continues to lick the calf, mooing softly. After a few minutes, the calf attempts to stand. Its back legs rise and reach relative stability. A long pause, and then it attempts to raise its front legs. It teeters, balancing perilously on two hind legs and two front knees. It falls. Mother continues to lick its legs.

I want to leave them alone. I also want to remove my coat, my cap, my gloves in the woods to prove that this January night may be chilly but not fatally cold. I turn off the flashlight and adjust to available light. And there is light reflected off the snow, but reflected from what? Stars? There is no sound, just the occasional whimper from mother cow.

I cross the fence out of the pasture and take the driveway home. No need for a flashlight now. Around the bend, lights of the house appear. Smoke rises straight from the chimney. No wind. Not even a breeze.

It's nine o'clock, and I calculate the Super Bowl game is over. I call neighbor Ray who is my resident expert on cattle matters. Ray answers the phone. No, the game is not over, two minutes to go, and his team has taken the lead. Despite that, he listens to my story and my question—should I bring the calf to the barn? His answer is no. The forecast is for a mild night, and Scottish Highland cattle are hardy. If the calf gets its first meal, it'll be fine. I agree and go back to reading until ten o'clock, when I make my final check before bed.

THAT REMINDS ME

The second check is less dramatic. My flashlight picks up the cow's eyes under the Norway pine. Standing beside her is the calf, legs braced to withstand mother's licks. I'm reminded of Robert Frost's poem "The Pasture."

> I'm going out to fetch the little calf that's standing by the mother.
> It's so young, it totters when she licks it with her tongue.
> I shan't be gone long. You come too.

Something tells me life will progress as it should here, with me or without me. The night is mild. The air is still.

I wake many times during the night trying to sense temperature changes. None. The image of the new calf, licked clean but licked wet and shivering, won't leave. At five-thirty, I rise and turn on the radio for the current temperature and forecast. Presently, sixteen degrees, with a high of twenty-eight predicted for today. What's more, continued unseasonably high temperatures throughout the week. I dress for my morning trek to the pasture. Stars shine, and there's a hint of light in the east.

I see the dark shape of the reclining cow under the Norway pine without a flashlight. There beside her, but not against her, is the calf. The cow turns her head toward me, and the calf lifts its head. It flicks its ears as if it hears me. The cow looks warm and comfortable; the calf has frosty spikes of licked hair. It holds its head high and watches.

Back at the house. I decide this memorable event must be commemorated. I brew a pot of coffee and consider an appropriate piece of music. Elgar's "Enigma Variations" comes to mind, specifically the "Nimrod Variation," appropriately named geographically. I sit before the fireplace and savor the moment. The power of animal instinct, the beauty of nature, the miracle of birth. The music rises in crescendo that lifts my already lifted spirit to tearful heights.

After breakfast, I make another visit to the bovine nativity scene. Both mother and baby are resting when I arrive and turn their heads toward me for the birth photograph. The calf stands, easily this time, and nudges mother. Mother stands, and the calf proceeds unerringly to the udder and sucks warm milk.

On the way to the house, I stop at the barnyard. One of last year's calves greets me at the haystack outside the fence. I give her news that she has a new brother or sister. No response. I walk into the barnyard and am greeted with a chorus of bellowing. "Yes, it's time for your morning feeding," I say, "but first I have news for you. You are now a herd of thirteen."

I walk to MacDuff. "You did yourself proud, Big Guy."

He nods to agree and presses me for morning grain.

SIXTH SENSE

You ask why I live by the river, alone
Well, do you know

The smell of linens bathed in summer sun
Heady smoke of jack pine fire in winter
Sun-thawed earth beside the house in spring

The sight of blue jays, blue as azure skies
Anemones that probe dead leaves, unfurl, and blossom
Galaxies that span horizons, north to south

The feel of velvet pussy willows
The roan foal's baby fur
Cool river skinny dips in summer

The sound of crunching leaves on trails
Coyote pups auditioning for choir
Muted conversations of white pines

The puck'ring taste of pin cherries
Wild morels when trillium bloom
Blueberries beside the pasture fence

And, do you know
My yearning when the collie barks
Your car negotiates the winding drive
I picked wild roses for the table

THAT REMINDS ME

BOUNDARY WATERS JOURNAL

Tuesday, September 1

5:05 AM. Time to rise after a fitful night of wind, rain, lightning, and thunder, my hopes dashed for one last night of sleep in a comfortable bed. First a shower, then the transport of luggage to the truck—one bag of personal stuff and another containing our kitchen. That, plus a two-man tent, rod and reel, and sleeping bag. Time to brew a fresh pot of coffee and drive to pick up teenaged grandson Peter.

At Lake Mitchell, Peter loads his luggage and sleeping bag, water purifier, maps, and two freeze-dried meals. "Just in case you get hungry," says Peter's dad/my son Greg in a well-intentioned but apprehensive voice.

Light rain falls at 7:30 as we strap the Old Town canoe atop the truck, and rain continues all morning. At McDonald's for breakfast in Duluth, we study Boundary Waters Canoe Area Wilderness (BWCAW) maps over coffee but defer a route decision until we hit water.

At 1 o'clock in the Grand Marais Ranger Station, Ranger Janet processes our BWCAW permit. But first we watch a ten-minute video of camping etiquette, do's and don'ts, precautions, and regulations. She hands us our permit after we pass a brief quiz to prove we paid attention. At the Holiday Station in town, we buy fishing licenses and sandwiches and head up the Gunflint Trail for a 40-minute drive. By now, clouds have cleared, the sun shines, and the temp feels mid-70s. We arrive at East Bearskin Lake and are on the water by 2 o'clock. We're energized by the crisp fall air and excited by the challenge.

We paddle east on Bearskin, hugging the south shore, watching for a designated campsite to confirm our map reading skills. The water is calm, and we pass two men fishing in a canoe. Motor boats are legal on this part of the lake, and we meet three boats. We identify a major land mass that splits the lake, and we cross to the north shore toward our first planned portage. The canoe is sturdy, stable, and quiet—a plastic resin model with comfortable molded seats.

Loons appear and disappear, some single, some in pairs. The lake is quiet, and the smooth ride is broken only by the spent wake of a passing pontoon. We move in tight to the north shore where we spot our first portage (unmarked) to Moon Lake.

The portage is our longest of the day, 115 rods, and sets a daunting precedent. We portage in two trips, carrying bags on trip one, the canoe on trip two. Unlike the calm flat lake, the trail climbs and descends, twists and turns, pitted with rocks and tree roots. We take a breather and confirm this is Moon Lake with other canoeists.

The Moon Lake experience is brief—a short paddle across the lake and a trip along the north shore, alert to the next portage to Deer Lake. We spot it on the first pass. Since the portage is short, 15 rods, we carry the loaded canoe, but give up.

The lakes in the BWCAW are long and narrow, east to west. The water is clear and weedless, with lake bottoms visible in ten feet depths.

We cross Deer Lake and canoe west along the north shore. By now, we can translate inches on the map to miles on the water. Deer Lake proves us wrong, or the cartographer misplaced the portage. It appears when we're ready to backtrack and take a second pass along the north shore. The portage from Deer Lake to Caribou Lake, our destination for today, is 60 rods. The first half is flat and rock-free; the second half is downhill and craggy. We portage in two trips again.

The woods are coniferous, with a healthy population of red cedar, Norway pine, spruce, and white birch. Raspberries are ripe. Wintergreen sprouts small red berries. Blue bead lilies sprout large blue berries. Cedar is the dominant aroma, complemented by heady moist forest floor. It rained the day before we arrived, but the sun shines today. It feels like 75 degrees at 5 o'clock when we arrive at the west end of Caribou Lake, exhausted but excited. This lake is home tonight, but only when we find a campsite.

Caribou hosts six campsites, all on the north side. The lake scales off at three miles, east to west. The first campsite is occupied by the group of three who passed us at Bearskin-Moon portage. The second site is occupied. So is the third. The fourth is a good distance, and we head for it with skepticism bordering on apprehension. It's occupied. The fifth is farther still, and we're tired from portaging and cramped from paddling. We spot what looks like an empty campsite, but it's occupied. One more site on this lake. We consider Plan B, and realize there is none. It's too late for another portage. The sun is dipping lower.

We head for the last campsite, in view. No luck; it's a portage. The final campsite is around the bend. It's in sight now, and no sign of occupancy. No canoe perched on the beach. No smoke rising from a campfire. No towels hanging from makeshift clotheslines. We're exhausted, too tired to talk. We paddle slowly, hoping against hope. Still no sign of occupancy. We glide to shore and spot a burning pit and no campfire. We stand, straighten and stretch tired bodies, and claim this site for Nimrod and Lake Mitchell.

The campsite nestles on a point with postcard lake views south and west. The new Gander Mountain tent erects in seconds, and a fire blazes minutes later, thanks to thoughtful campers who left mossy twigs and branches. It's 7 o'clock. The air is warm, the sky clear. A sliver of moon appears in the southwest. A loon cries. Smoke from the fire pit shifts south to west, then east. Waves lap easily at the shore. This is camp. This is home. We decide to make it permanent and take a day trip tomorrow rather than forego this choice site.

At 9 o'clock, we crash after a light dinner of roast pork and cheese sandwiches on English muffins, washed down by Tang and followed by dessert of granola bars. Sleep is sporadic, but rest is good. I pry open one eye during the night and see stars through nylon screening, so close I can reach them. I listen for the call of a loon, and sleep.

Wednesday, September 2

6:30 AM. I rise and Peter sleeps. I maneuver out of the sleeping bag, muscles stiff and aching, and head for the fire pit to start the breakfast fire. Peter has purified a supply of water for coffee and Tang. In time, the percolator is gurgling. The aroma of hot coffee complements the wood crackling in the fire pit.

Across the lake, tips of trees are ignited by the rising sun. I walk with my coffee cup to water's edge. An intricate spider web with microdots of dew spans the narrow path. Minnows spot my arrival, flap their tails, and dive, leaving a dozen concentric rings. Small beetles with neon blue bodies alight on a sunken log. Water bugs assemble, then mix and disperse with dizzying speed, randomly rushing, like the world we left behind.

At 8 o'clock, Peter rises and we consider breakfast—pancakes dotted with trail mix. An abundance of birch bark and downed birch trees makes good kindling. Beaver-gnawed driftwood smolders and creates hot embers. We add pine boughs for aroma. With twice as much batter as we need, we make one huge final pancake, a potential peace offering for Papa Bear.

We high-five our cooking on the wood-fired grill. The only issue is carbon buildup on pots and pans, but since the cookware was a one-dollar garage sale purchase, what's the problem?

After breakfast, Peter settles in a fallen tree formation on the point and reads. I snap a Rapala on my line and cast off the west shore into a rocky bay. I feel two strikes and hook a small walleye. Conclusion: there are fish in this bay, Rapala is the right lure, and fish feed at 10 o'clock.

The rest of the morning is hiking, reading, exploring, writing, swimming, and attempting to capture the elusive beauty of the Boundary Waters on film. After lunch, I nap. Peter reads. Later, I take the canoe into the bay. A breeze from the east chops the water, but I'm able to execute a decent cast. In time, I catch and release two small walleyes. Conclusion confirmed.

Lack of sleep the previous night and grueling portages catch up with me. I take a second nap. Peter reads on.

Hints of autumn appear—red woodbine hugging a pine tree, a cool north breeze with a bite, yellow birches along the spine of island ridges. I slip into a sweatshirt.

Later in the afternoon, the breeze dies, and we canoe to the east end of the lake to catch dinner. The canoe glides across still water, slicing a clean V on the surface. After a few casts, a northern pike snake strikes. As fast as the wind died, it resurrects, and we head for our home bay. After a few more casts, I get a strike and set the hook. The fish clears the water, a good-sized walleye. There's our meal. I land him, and we head for shore.

Dinner that night is pan-fried walleye and instant potatoes fried with onions. Clearly five-star Michelin. One fish is the right amount. In addition to being delicious, the fish dinner is a victory for us. We avoid freeze-dried meals.

We have no radio or cell phones. No way of hearing news of the BWCAW fire at the north end of Gunflint Trail. We smell no smoke and see no haze in the north sky.

Bedtime arrives early, and after a quick dip in the lake, we plan to weigh anchor early the next morning.

Thursday, September 3

5:30 AM. I rise, crank up the fire, and boil a pot of coffee. Peter rises at six for a breakfast of grilled English muffins with cheese and a cup of Tang. He packs the tent; I pack the kitchen. We launch the canoe for our trip home by 6:30, opting for a similar route with one variation at the end which adds one lake and one portage.

Fog has set in and conceals the opposite shore. The sun lingers on the east horizon. The lake is mirror calm. Fog accentuates the silence; the only sound is the dip of paddles. The view is water, shrouded trees, and rocks. This is the essence of the Boundary Waters. A spoken word is a violation; a floating wrapper is a capital offense. We hug the south shore of Caribou Lake while a pallid wafer of sun rises and penetrates the fog. We plan a one-hour ride and make it in 55 minutes. It's an easy portage to Deer Lake. Campsites must be full, because a group of canoeists camps at the portage site.

We paddle across Deer Lake to the long portage to Moon Lake where we head for the west end. The portage is a testy trip with a mud patch at the onset, followed by a rocky climb. Along the way, I hear a murmur, then a ripple of water. A spring-fed stream trickles down the hill beside our path. I splash cool, fresh water on my sweating face and arms, and drink. On the top of the hill are plentiful patches of raspberries, attesting to this not being a popular trail. We enjoy a second breakfast.

Our new route takes us to Flour Lake. We need only to canoe west along a peninsula and then back east to the final portage to East Bearskin. Flour Lake allows motorized boats, and we see and hear Modern Times again. In two days of wilderness, we've acclimated to the quiet life. The speed, size, and noise of power boats are offensive. I fight an urge to paddle faster to distance myself from them.

The last portage is the most difficult. It splits at the top of a hill with no sign indicating which direction leads to East Bearskin. The mix-up costs us a half hour, but we are on East Bearskin at 11:55 for the last leg of our odyssey. Canoe traffic is heavy heading back, like aircraft lined up for landing. We hit the ramp at the parking area at 12:55, load our gear and canoe, and head down the Gunflint Trail for Grand Marais.

The adventure was our opportunity to connect—grandfather to grandson; to know each other, and ourselves, better. Gratifying for me to learn that love of outdoors, love of active recreation, love of reading permeate our genetics. An adventure like this is best enjoyed in the company of the young. Their exuberance and willingness to prove they can pull their own weight often compels them to do more than their share. Portaging the canoe, for example. The portages were a challenge, but the weekend was, for the most part, relaxing.

I'll remember the unspoiled beauty of the shoreline. The rush and relief of finding the last campsite on Caribou. The silence of fog. The mirror image reflection of pines and cedars along the shore. The morning campfire smoke rising through shafts of sunlight in the pines, like incense in a cathedral.

JED MUELLER'S AUCTION

November seven, oatmeal morning
Pale sun squints through frosted branches
Highway signs warn *Auction Traffic*
Neighbors migrate to Jed Mueller's

Pickup trucks along the driveway
park in hay fields, spill on roads.
Get your bidding number, Mister,
at the purple trailer there

Men blow steam and nod *g'mornin'*
tuck gloved hands behind their bibs.
Coffee, rolls at Toby's wagon
cash or check, no credit cards

Ninety-three year old Jed Mueller
takes a day leave from Rest Haven
Greets the neighbors from his pickup
turns to hear above the speakers

Flatbed wagons piled with relics
rusted remnants, horse-drawn days
Harness, collars, planters, pickers
four dump rakes along the fence

Five draft horses
One. One. Do I hear a thousand?
Jed cranes and listens. Says goodbye
He nods and naps

The truck is last.
Going. Going. Going.
Gone.

THAT REMINDS ME

SHELTER BELT

Mid-morning in the middle of Montana, Big Sky country. The Empire Builder conductor announces the dining car is closed for breakfast. Through a film of window grime, a monotonous winter gray stretches west over bland prairie to a blurry horizon. Utility poles rush by the window, standing at attention like a miles-long honor guard. A herd of whitetails scampers off the siding and scatters toward nowhere, everywhere, anywhere.

Single passengers in double seats curl up, stretch out, twist like pretzels in impromptu sleep positions. Of those awake, a gray-haired man ahead hums as he reads. A young woman across the aisle watches a movie. Forward a couple seats, a gravel-voiced wildcatter talks on his phone telling his woman, and the world, how anxious he is to get home. "The first thing we're gonna do is make love," he says. "Then I'll put down my duffle bag."

"I tell you, man. It ain't easy," comes a chirpy voice from behind. Then a fake chuckle, like a cornered man in a tight spot. "It ain't easy and it ain't gonna get easier." Another chuckle. "I've been dry for four years. Four years, three months, ten days." Chuckle. He pauses. "And twelve minutes. It ain't easy."

Outside, an unbroken landscape of grain stubble shelters random patches of snow. A tar road appears, like a black marker line stretching to infinity. Last night small town streetlamps interrupted the barren blackness every twenty, thirty miles standing like magical matchsticks. On the parallel ribbon of highway, a semitrailer flaunting multi-colored lights played tag with the train, outpaced it, and disappeared. This morning, the barren landscape copes with the cruel reality of daylight.

"You think you're hurting now, Bro. Wait 'til tomorrow. And tomorrow." Chirp, and then the irritating chuckle. "And tomorrow." He drums the seatback with his fingers. "But you did the right thing, Bro. You got out of there before you killed yourself."

The sun's pale eye sneaks over the clouds and stares through the window. Off to the right, a windbreak of fir trees wraps its arms around a modest bungalow, its chimney exhaling a hefty ribbon of white smoke. At the barn, horses jaw on hay behind a corral fence of poles. A pickup idles in the driveway. A sign at the mailbox says *Holm Sweet Home.*

"You traveling light," comes the voice with a chuckle. "What you leaving behind?"

"Nothin'," in a low frightened voice.

"No car? No house? No job? No woman?"

"Maybe a woman."

"Maybe?"

"She wasn't my woman. Like, we weren't married or anything."

"Does she know you're gone?"

"She will."

An oncoming freight screams its approach and thunders past within arm's length. Pale sunlight between the gaps of cars flashes like strobe lights.

"Four years for me. Can't say I don't miss the stuff. But I'm alive." Chirp and chuckle. "Alive and well. And I wouldn't be if I were still using. You think it's gonna be easy? It ain't."

"What's your secret?" comes the second voice in clipped, soft words.

"Secret? No secret. You have to work that out for yourself." He parks his tray table in the seatback. "But you're off to a great start. What did she do to turn your crank?"

"Who said she did anything?" His voice is protective, as if a part of him is back with her.

"I've been around the block a few times. I know women. She did something."

"She kicked me out last night. Meth makes her mean. I'm sitting on the stoop at 3 AM this morning, freezing my ass, and wondering what the hell I'm doing here."

"A freezing ass is a powerful motivator."

"I walked back in, grabbed a few clothes and my jacket and headed for the depot."

"Smart man. You could've stuck around and watched her kill herself. Like my sister did. And my half-brother. And my uncle and three cousins."

"Your attention, please," drawls the PA system. "The snack bar below the observation car is now open for hot and cold sandwiches, chips, candy bars, soft drinks, and beer. Y'all come, hear?"

42

"I wish she'd stop talking about food." Chuckle. "And beer."

"Amen."

"How far you heading, Bro?"

"Tacoma."

"You got family there? Some support system?"

"Don't know a soul. It's as far as I could go on the cash I lifted from her drug money."

"Her world is a powerhouse, Bro. Don't be surprised if you have a welcome party at the Tacoma depot." He makes a squishy noise, like slitting a throat.

"I'll take the chance."

"First thing you do is find a social worker. Ask for a sponsor. You'll never make it without a sponsor. You may not make it with a sponsor." Chuckle. "It's bad stuff. And when you're done looking for it, it'll look for you. Sobriety is a house of cards."

The train brakes with a jolt and slows. Far ahead, the engine wails like a lost dog and crawls through an isolated hamlet resembling the backlot of a B movie studio. Monolithic grain storage buildings with rusted tin siding hug the tracks. A flock of pigeons circles the loading dock. A school bus waits at the single crossing, its yellow warning lights synchronized with the ding-ding-ding of the railroad semaphores.

Downtown streets are bare. Little square houses run parallel with the track, a downspout dangling here, a screen door swinging there. A clear plastic bag waves from the barbed wire fence separating houses from tracks. Abandoned cars and trucks snuggle in backyard snowbanks.

A conductor walks down the aisle checking boarding tickets. "Welcome aboard," she says to the two. "How far you gents going with us today?" She is a small, black woman, curly gray hair, looking months, weeks from retirement.

"I'm going to Wolf Creek. He's going to Tacoma."

"Tacoma? You've got a long ride ahead of you, friend." She places seat checks on the overhead luggage racks.

"That's what I told him. It's a long way to Tacoma."

"Leaving home? Going home?" She seems to address the quiet man.

"He's making a break. Leaving his nasty-tongued woman. And he's leaving some of her bad habits. I told him it ain't gonna be easy."

"Are you his guardian?"

"Hell, no. I just met him in Rugby."

THAT REMINDS ME

"Is this your ticket?" she asks. "Ah, Aaron. A good biblical name."

"And I'm Leonard," the chatty one adds. "Lucky Leonard, they call me."

"Aaron, what're you making a break from?" Her voice is calm, caring.

"His woman is hooked on some bad stuff. He busted out this morning. Spent the family inheritance on a train ticket. And here he is."

"Aaron, what're you running from?"

A meek voice answers, "I guess he about summed it up."

"One final try, Aaron. What're you running from?"

"Bad drugs. Bad habits. Bad people."

"That's better. You gotta name your demons before you can conquer them." Her voice softens. "How long you been straight?"

"He's got all of a half day. Me, I've got four years and counting. I told him it ain't easy."

The young woman across the aisle rises and throws a disapproving glance.

"Who's waiting for you in Tacoma, Aaron? You got family there?"

"I asked him the same question, didn't I, Bro? You gotta have a support system. You'll never make it on your own."

"Aaron, who's waiting for you in Tacoma?"

"No one."

"Well, you'll need somebody. Somebody waiting for you. Tacoma is my hometown. Maybe I can help you find some social services there."

"I told him the same thing, didn't I, Bro? First thing. Get yourself a sponsor. Before you get a room. Before you get a meal. First thing you get a sponsor."

"Aaron, listen to me." Her voice is faint, like a whisper. "I want you to listen to me. I care about you and so does God. He loves you so much, He gave His Son Jesus to give you a new life. The past is forgiven. The future is bright. All you have to do is believe. Believe and accept Jesus as your personal Savior. Have you done that? Have you accepted Jesus as your personal Savior?"

Silence. Then, "I'm not sure."

"Well, do it. Even your sponsor won't be at your side 24/7. Jesus will. You call him anytime. His line is never busy. You understand what I'm saying?"

"I guess so."

"I told him it ain't easy. I know. Four years, and it still ain't easy."

"I'm a single mom," she says, "and I saw my son through his trials and tribulations. It's not easy, but in the long run, it's worth it."

"That's what I told him. It ain't easy."

The young woman across the aisle returns with a takeout carton. When she opens the cover, the aroma of onions and Italian sausage floods the area.

"Damn," a voice whispers.

"Aaron, would you mind if I laid my hand on your shoulder and prayed with you?"

No response.

"All loving and all powerful God," she prays. "Look down on your new servant Aaron. Help him in his hour of need. He can't do it without you, Lord. Please, please, have mercy on his troubled soul. Amen."

And an echo, "Amen."

"Excuse me a few minutes," the conductor says.

An oncoming freight train screams alongside, its black oil cars like a mile-long pipeline. The coach car sways; wheels clack and clatter. In a swish, the final freight car disappears.

The conductor returns with two lunch cartons. "They give me way too much food. Care to share it with me?"

The humming reader ahead must have heard the conversation. When the conductor walks past, he reaches for her arm. "You're a good woman," he says. "God bless you."

A brief smile washes across her face.

Back in the coach car after lunch, the men have separated. Both lie, their heads leaning against windows, their jackets bunched into pillows. Both lace their fingers across their bellies. Both breathe deep and relaxed, safe in the temporal shelter of sleep.

THAT REMINDS ME

ICE OUT
Homage to Irene

Plates of crystal float the winter river
in grave procession, miles long
they grind and grate and scrape the shore.
Scraps of life—a root, a branch, a reed.

Somber, solemn ceremony
An endless cortege day to night
Wailing, moaning night to day
Mourners to a mute command.

What mortal's so revered?
What hero, head of state, what saint
commands this honor?

Listen
Ice glides against the frozen shore
and wails a cold discordant dirge.

NOVEMBER: SHERBURNE COUNTY

In late 1941, in the Minnesota countryside, old men stared into the face of war. News reports crackled from the radio of invasions in Poland, atrocities in Czechoslovakia, bombing raids in London.

Only the children were optimistic. For them, life was predictable—chores morning and night, school homework, the promise of Christmas. The turmoil across the ocean resembled a history lesson, a romantic adventure. Another country, another planet, another world.

Their farmhouse was modest—L-shaped, once painted, tucked behind an unruly orchard and tethered to barns and sheds by winding dirt paths. Inside, a Monarch wood stove loomed like a kitchen throne: six burner plates, water reservoirs on either side, a warming oven across the top, firewood stacked vertically in a charred box, and the incessant aroma of wood smoke.

The living room housed the pot-bellied heater, the dinner table and chairs, a maroon frieze sofa and easy chair, a radio. Against the north wall, between windows that looked out to the orchard and woodpile, a piano. An upright Kimball piano, looking misplaced, lost, like a tuxedoed dandy at a barn dance. Atop the piano, a sepia photograph of a soldier.

At night before supper, the woman led the family in prayer. *Bless us, O Lord . . .* and at the end, she added, *and please God, protect our Robert.*

After supper, the man took his chair beside the radio, cupped his ear, and listened to the news. The woman sat on the sofa beneath a floor lamp, darning socks. "Oh, Harold," she said. "Turn it off. It's so depressing."

Kids leaned over the dinner table, their heads buried in history books, arithmetic, and spelling, jotting notes on Chief tablets. All but a young girl, who sat at the piano feeling her way through "Claire de

Lune" with a soft touch, beneath the sound of the newscast.

Days were warm for November, but winter hid behind the door like a bratty kid. *Remember me?* it said. After school, while older brothers and sisters milked cows and fed calves, the boy and girl pulled a milk can in a wagon to the pump and filled it for tomorrow. The girl washed her hands with pine tar soap in an enamel basin beside the door and set the table for supper. The boy split wood and carried it from the woodpile for the overnight fire.

The girl finished her table setting and sat at the piano. She retraced her way through "Claire de Lune" and began Chopin's "Prelude in E-minor," a song she learned from an RCA record on the Victrola.

What's a prelude? the boy wondered.

Music wafted from the open window as if to drive reality away. A south breeze carried the tune to the woodpile, to the boy. He stopped. "Prelude," he said, and let music and moment congeal.

HEATWAVE

May is like that. A random heatwave kicks the ass of winter in one sultry afternoon. The sun kisses us awake like Sleeping Beauties after a long winter's nap. Such is Donna as she lies on her blanket behind the apartment house, her toddler aligning toy cars on the blanket stripe and her baby asleep in a bassinette shaded from the afternoon sun by newspaper. A portable radio plays jazzy music from the college radio station.

Willard walks from the parking lot behind the apartment house, an armful of books on one side, a key chain swinging from his finger on the other. It's Friday, and it's spring. An earthy aroma from the south-facing garden floods the yard, and a balmy breeze tickles the skin.

"Hi there," Donna calls. "All done for the week?"

Willard has seen this woman before, bundled in a winter jacket, struggling through the front door with a twin stroller. Or balancing a bag of groceries on one hip, a baby on the other, her key poking at the front door lock. Now, halter straps dangle from her shoulders. She lies on her stomach, a magazine curled in her hand.

"All done," he says. "Very warm for May."

"I'm Donna, 104," she says. "And these are my children. What college are you in? What year?"

"Just wrapping up my freshman year. Pre-business. And you?"

"My husband Paul is a professional grad student, working on his second masters. We're the proverbial poor student family." She chuckles. "Don't even have a car."

"Well," Willard stumbles, "if you ever need transportation, I can help."

"I might take you up on that. And I didn't catch your name."

"Willard."

"Willard?" She smiles. "I'll call you Willy. Nice to meet you,

Willy."

He walks into the house, up the stairs to his apartment. From the hall window, he sees her lift the newspaper from the sleeping baby. The toddler eats Cheerios from a small box. She slides sunglasses down from her hair and returns to the magazine.

The first heatwave of summer wears on. Willard looks for the woman and her children on weekend afternoons. Nothing. Her brashness intrigues him, invites his imagination into mysterious entanglements. Older women are known to seek young men; he knows that. And how old is she? Thirty, plus or minus? He hates to guess a woman's age.

Monday after classes, he sees her again in the backyard with the children.

"Willy," she calls. "I hope you were serious about your offer of transportation. Would you be willing to drive me on a short shopping trip Wednesday afternoon? I'll pay for gas." She lifts herself off the blanket and slides her shoulder straps up.

"Sure, I could help." Willard feels a tingle, a strange shock of confidence, an air of superiority that comes with giving.

She stands and touches his arm. "I'd like that," she says. The smile he remembers crosses her face. "About this time on Wednesday? I'll be ready. Just knock on the door."

He looks for her later in the day, walks by 104 hoping to see her, wondering what he'll say if he bumps into her grad student husband. Will he know of the transportation offer?

Willard washes the car, empties the ashtrays, whisks the floor carpets. He remembers a blanket in the trunk, shakes it, and folds it in the back seat. He puts a Glen Campbell tape in the player. If they end up in his apartment, there's beer in the fridge and a couple shots of gin. If it comes to that.

On Wednesday, Willard parks his car on the street in front of the apartment, dusts the dashboard with his sleeve, and lifts the armrest that separates the driver from the front seat passenger. He checks his image in the window and proceeds to 104. He hears "Come in," and opens the door. She stands by the couch, strapping the baby in a car seat. The toddler licks a sucker and tugs at her skirt hem. "We'll be ready in a minute," she says. "I do appreciate this."

"The kids . . .?" Willard blurts, and regrets asking it.

52

"This trip is so important to me," she says. "I'll make it up to you, I swear."

In the car, she straps the boy in the back seat and slides into the front seat with the baby. "Thanks," she smiles as he closes the door.

"Where to?"

"1310 West 28th Street. It's a pawn shop."

"Redeeming the wedding silverware?"

"Nope. Hocking some old meaningless jewelry. Old engagement rings, gifts from people who disappeared from my life."

The boy in the back seat cries when he drops his sucker. She turns to retrieve it for him and braces her hand on Willard's leg. "There," she says to the boy. "Now is everybody happy?" And then, "Do you have a girlfriend, Willy?"

"Yes, kind of. Linda. She's still in high school."

"Oh, that's too bad." Willard detects a tease in her voice. Like still in high school is kid stuff, inexperienced.

At the pawn shop, Donna hands the baby to him. "This won't take long," she says. "I really appreciate your help. I'll make it up to you."

So this is what domestic life is all about, Willard thinks. Chauffeur. Baby sitter. Where's the romance?

Back home, she invites him into her apartment. "I have a pitcher of iced tea waiting," she says. "Go ahead and pour a couple glasses while I put the little guy down for his nap."

When she returns from the bedroom, she lifts her glass and clinks against his. "To friendship." The baby squeals in her infant seat.

"She's hungry," Donna says. "Would it embarrass you if I breastfed her?" She lifts the baby from the seat, places a towel over her shoulder and over the baby's head, and wriggles a breast from her blouse. She sits on the couch, Willard beside her.

"I suppose you're wondering about my excitement," she says. "Next week is our tenth anniversary. I want to buy Paul a ring. I can't tell you how much I love that man."

Willard sighs and feels his ego implode. "Does Paul know about us?" he asks. "I mean about our transportation arrangement?"

"Yes," she says. She lifts her hand from her breast and places it on his arm and smiles. "I told him he can trust you."

Years later, when Willard and Linda attend a pre-marriage

THAT REMINDS ME

retreat, the facilitator asks each couple to find a quiet spot and tell the intimate details of their lives, confess their sins so to speak. "If you can't trust your partner with your past, you can't trust them with your future."

Willard relates the Donna story, the attraction, the infatuation, the sexual fantasy.

"But she was married," Linda says. "She had two kids. She was almost ten years older than you. What were you thinking?"

Willard is quiet. It was May, he remembers, and the first heatwave of summer.

OVERHEARD AT THE GAS PUMP

Ya know what I mean? Huh? Ya know what I mean? It don't make no difference. Ya pay two-fifty a gallon for regular gas and three-fifty for premium. Guess what? It all comes out of the same tank. Ya know what I mean? It's the damn oil companies that are makin' all the money. Ya know what I mean? Talk about price fixin'. Three gas stations in town, and they all charge the exact same price. Down to a tenth of a cent, for chrisakes. Don't tell me that ain't collusion. Ya know what I mean? Huh? Just watch now. They'll bump up the price when Christmas starts. Ya know how I know? Because they do the same goddamn thing for Easter. And the Fourth of July. And Labor Day. I'm tellin' ya, they got the whole shittin' batch of politicians in their pocket. Us little bastards don't stand a chance. Ya know what I mean? I'm tellin' ya, this world is goin' to hell in a handbasket. Ya know what I mean? Huh? Ya know what I mean?

IN MEMORIAM: PRESIDENT GERALD R. FORD

Gerald Ford, 38th President, Dies at 93
New York Times headline, December 27, 2006

Sunday, September 8, 1974. A group of political candidates gathered at a coffee party in Spring Park, Minnesota, to relish recent polling results and glow in the prospects of election in November. I was the Republican-endorsed candidate for the State House of Representatives, District 42A, the western edge of Hennepin County. At a seasoned 42 years of age, I ran strong opposition to the 23-year old incumbent who was born the year I began my lifetime career at Honeywell.

On the national scene, President Richard Nixon had resigned the month before rather than face impeachment following the Watergate scandal. President Nixon had appointed Michigan Congressman Gerald Ford as Vice President after Spiro Agnew resigned amid another scandal. Upon Mr. Nixon's resignation, Vice President Ford assumed the presidency. Domestic politics were in high turmoil.

We milled in the party room of the Spring Park apartment house when news broke of President Ford's pardon of Mr. Nixon. *We interrupt this program to bring you an important news bulletin.* President Ford spoke with conviction, sincerity, and humility.

I have come to a decision which I felt I should tell you and all of my fellow American citizens, as soon as I was certain in my own mind and in my own conscience that it is the right thing to do.

I wasn't a political pro, this being my first run for state office. But I knew this pardon, well-intentioned and reasonable, was the kiss of death to my candidacy and to the entire Republican slate in Minnesota and the nation.

In his memoirs, President Ford wrote that he hoped the pardon would be seen as an act of courage. It was seen as an act of impulse or worse, as an act of settling a deal: I appoint you as Vice President and then resign; you assume the Presidency and grant me full pardon. As much as I admired the new President, it was a leap of faith not to assume the latter.

I met Gerald Ford as Vice President in the summer of 1974. He was a guest of State Senator and Mrs. George Pillsbury at their home in Wayzata. Mrs. Betty Ford, nee Elizabeth Bloomer, had a sibling in Wayzata which prompted the Minnesota visit. Candidates for local, state, and national office were invited to meet the Vice President and pose for the requisite campaign photograph. That gave me a minute, face to face, with this great man. What to say? My issues in District 42A were peanuts compared to the issues facing the nation—inflation, a depressed economy, energy shortages, riven politics, the communist threat in southeast Asia. I settled on education, with an attempt to sound both erudite and humble. He listened with saintly patience. It's informative that the photograph shows me talking and the Vice President listening.

In November, the electorate confirmed my intuition. I did well as a first time candidate against an incumbent, but lost by a healthy seven-point margin. We called it a Republican blood bath. Yes, all politics are local, except those which are national.

Not to sound like a rationalization, but I thank President Ford for his bold action. He initiated a national healing process which contributed to my loss in 1974 and his in 1976. Career politics wasn't in the cards for either of us. I also thank him for my loss. A win would have led me to aspire to the State Senate and Congress. I am not wired for the demands and scrutiny of a political life.

REFLECTIONS ON THE WATER

Legend has it Paul Bunyan rose from his lodge in Akeley one day with a plan to walk south and view the timber supply. His mighty footprint created a lake, then another, then another. By the time he reached Huntersville, eleven footprints drained the countryside and created eleven lakes. While he scoured the area for old growth timber, the lakes filled, then overflowed, connecting one to another. They continued to rise while Paul scanned the ample varieties and quantities of cordage. With nowhere to go, the overflow formed a river. Paul watched his creation and noted the new river twisting and turning in gentle arcs. "Like a raven wing," he said to Babe. "But, you know, crow wing is easier to say."

Fast forward to 2015. The river continues to flow from the eleven Crow Wing Lakes, meandering, rising, and falling with the seasons. Now it's January and the river is frozen. The constant, soothing flow of water is on hold, at least on the surface. Beneath a plate of ice, another world exists. Water courses at a constant five miles an hour, silvery minnows dart to nowhere and, beneath them in primordial mud, turtles and frogs shut down for the winter.

Four o'clock Sunday afternoon, and the day's temperature tops out at -7 F. Cattle are impervious to the cold and poke their heads into the bale feeder like spokes in a wheel. The flag at the river hangs limp, then flutters to life at the north wind's provocation. The dog senses it's walking time and runs down the bank, chancing the thickness of ice. On the river, a scrim of virgin snow billows and collects in miniature contours. No snowmobile tracks outline the shore; open water is reported at bridges.

A pale wafer of sun seems ready to call it a day as we follow the river north. Tawny gold grass trembles and complements our long blue shadows on the snow. At the oxbow which defines the farm boundary, black ash bend and lock branches in ice, victims of last summer's winds. It's quiet and desolate. No footprints, hoof prints, paw prints.

The walk back to the house follows the river through the woods, also quiet and desolate. As the muted sun lowers, it creates miniature pastel prisms in the snow. Soon a hint of jack pine wood smoke. Closer, it's a welcome aroma. Chickadees flutter at the feeder. A nuthatch scolds. A woodpecker drums a tiny solo.

Visitors have remarked on the beauty of the river and its environs in spring, summer, and fall. In spring, the joy of water fowl migration and budding dogwood. In summer, the parade of exuberant high school seniors canoeing on a class trip; a pair of swans lazing in the bay. In fall, congregating Canada geese, the incredible redness of high bush cranberries. *But doesn't winter's cold become life threatening?* they ask. *Don't you feel lonesome and deserted in winter?*

No.

As Emerson declaims, *Indeed, the river is a perpetual gala, and boasts each month a new ornament.* There is no peace like the river and woods in winter. No scene as simple and beautiful as dichromatic trees and snow. No destination as welcome as warm yellow lights of home on a moonlit night, fresh snow frosting the Norway pines, wood smoke curling from the chimney. And from across the river, coyotes howling and owls hooting in raucous conversation.

A visiting archaeologist commented that the features which attract us to this spot on the river are the same as those that attracted Native Americans—a panoramic view up and down the river, not for aesthetics but for defense, and the river on three sides of the oxbow which permits efficient game drives. Dig a foot of riverbank topsoil, he said, and you'll find artifacts.

Let them be.

A visiting geologist remarked upon inspecting an aerial photograph that the river has changed course. At one time it flowed straight across the base of the oxbow. A riverbed of rocks in the pasture confirmed that.

The water flowing past the farm converges with the Long Prairie at Motley, the Mississippi at Pillager, the Gulf of Mexico at New Orleans. From there our modest Minnesota waters mix with the big guys—the Caribbean Sea, the Atlantic Ocean, and through the Panama Canal, the Pacific. Our humble river, the one that consoles and cools, inspires and indulges, connects Nimrod to the planet.

Years ago a neighbor, also impressed with this connectivity, floated 35mm film cartridges containing his business cards in the river. A note on the back of the cards read, *Return this to the address on the front*. A couple miles downstream from where he made his deposit, the Crow Wing makes an improbable bend to the north. The reluctant river hangs back, creating a backwater bay along the farm shore. The cartridges floated that far, then snagged in foliage and bobbed among shafts of wild rice. Traveling friends, eager to collaborate in a little mischief, wrote letters and mailed them from Florida, Hawaii, all the way from Normandy Beach. Improbable yes, but possible. The perpetrator was not identified, until now.

Literature is replete with rivers as metaphors for interconnectedness and constancy of change. Greek philosopher Heraclitus promoted change as being central to the universe. *No man ever steps in the same river twice, for it's not the same river, and he's not the same man.* Twenty-five-hundred years later, Ralph Waldo Emerson wrote: *Man is a stream whose source is hidden.* And, *Who looks upon a river in a meditative hour and is not reminded of the flux of all things?* Finally . . . *But blood rolls uninterruptedly an endless circulation through all men as the water of the globe is all one sea and truly seen, its tide is one.*

REFRACTIONS

Creative Fiction

AND A BIER FOR DAD

So here I am, walking up the church aisle again, this time behind the widow instead of in front of the bride. I was flower girl when she married my dad thirty-five years ago, so happy to be part of the wedding, to wear my new organdy dress with eyelet ribbons and tiny buttons. Happy until I saw her daughters, junior bridesmaids, in long satin gowns.

That day years ago, my stepmother wore a white gown; today, she wears gray wool. Her walk is the same—unsteady then in white heels, unsteady now in black Hush Puppies. She leans into the daughter beside her, the surviving daughter. The other, dead from an overdose years ago, was sent to The Great Beyond with a quiet funeral mass attended by family and a few tattooed fellow travelers.

Today, the front pews are occupied, the center of the church empty, the rear a haphazard array of singles. Although it's September, the church feels like a giant walk-in cooler—vacant, damp, cold.

I recognize Dad's fishing buddies in their black rayon Al's Bait Shop jackets, his fellow union members from Federal Cartridge, the Knights of Columbus honor guard in creased white shirts and navy polyester pants. What are they doing here? Dad wasn't a KC. I smell coffee brewing in the basement, and suddenly crave caffeine.

Look at the morning sun glint through the stained glass windows. Look at the brilliant patches of greens and reds and blues on the white shirts of the KCs and on the white banners—*Husband* and *Father*, draped on the coffin. Look at the bouquets and wreaths that dot the altar. Why these? This group of mourners doesn't look prosperous enough to afford them. Why the expensive casket? Why the funeral mass, for God's sake? I think I know who funded this party. We all have an image to protect.

The organist struggles with "Nearer My God to Thee." I think "Another One Bites the Dust." At my stepsister's funeral, the ushers passed the collection plate. Dad said it would be a cold day in Hell before he went back to this church. Maybe I should call him and ask about the temperature down there.

The priest reminded my stepmother at the wake last night that he will ask for reminiscences of the departed during the funeral mass. I pray that she resisted the temptation. She's honed a litany of husbandly and fatherly attributes over the last few days. Before they married, did he really offer his house to her when she was evicted from her apartment? Did he really give her the keys to his pickup when her car was repossessed? And the rose story—a fresh rose every day in the truck, on the front door knob of the house, on her desk at the Credit Union. Was that true? Who cares? Remind me to never trust a man who sends a rose every day.

Dad. We achieved our final degree of separation the day he lit up a Marlboro in my baby's bedroom. I grabbed the cigarette, bumped the beer bottle out of his hand, and gave him the choice of reprogramming his bad habits or staying away. He didn't return.

So here we are, the "survived by . . ." crowd. We take our seats in the front pew. The priest walks from the altar, forces a lame smile, and reaches for my stepmother's hand. I'm embarrassed and touch the hem of my leather skirt, tugging it to my knees. The priest wears a white damask stole with intricately embroidered red-orange flames. I want to touch the flames, feel the fire. Is this the Holy Spirit? Or are these the eternal flames of Hell? My stepmother lifts her hand. Her wedding ring rotates on her skinny finger. "God be with you," the priest says.

She whimpers a tinny "Thank you." He holds her hand, chalky paper skin, burrowed veins, bony knuckles. She manages a tentative smile and heaves a sigh that trembles her body.

Suddenly I pity her, her life dictated and defined by someone else. Harvey's wife, Harvey's widow, the "little woman," as he called her in his drunken stupors. Forty years at the Credit Union, keeping the family afloat while he drifted from job to job. His binge drunks, the night he fell against the heirloom china cabinet and smashed the door and half her grandmother's china. Her broken arm when she fell down the stairs, if you could believe her. And in the last months, her frustration at his ignoring the doctor's death warnings if he veered from his medication regimen.

Is there a grin behind her grimace? Does she think *good riddance*?

She must have loved him. Or needed the pain. Or couldn't accept living alone. Who cares? If it's good enough for her, it's good enough for me. At least someone will be praying for him.

The priest intones. "In the name of the Father, and of the Son, and of the Holy Spirit."

"Amen."

HITCH

Minnesota 210 *is a highway that spans the northern wooded half of the state, from Breckenridge on the South Dakota line to Oliver, Wisconsin, eight miles south of Superior. A stretch in Aitkin County is named Dale Wayrynen Memorial Highway, in honor of a local soldier who gave his life in Vietnam to save his comrades. On an uninhabited ten-mile stretch between McGregor and Tamarack, a woman walks.*

Damn, damn, damn. I had to get out of that car. Get away from him, his rage. He would have killed me. Where the hell am I? This country's deserted. Trees and trees and more trees. No buildings, no mailboxes, not even a telephone pole. He's heading for the casino, with or without me, trying to beat the morning rush. Maybe I should head back to the house, grab a few things, and be out of here. For good.

Looks like a pedestrian ahead. It is. A woman. Walking. Hitching a ride. Out here in the middle of nowhere. Didn't see a stalled car along the road or one nosed in the ditch. She's waving. Swinging a bag. Wearing a jogging suit. Too far from anywhere to be jogging. Must be five miles back to town, another five to the next one. What the hell?

Here comes a car. Sun's in my eyes. Can't see if there's anyone in the passenger seat. Hey, slow down, slow down. Damsel in distress ahead. Please. Please. Help me get away before he turns around to get me. He'll run me off the road, I know. I'm sure you can see me.

Wonder what's going on. Doesn't look good. You hear about creeps that hitch a ride, then take your money or your car or your life. Or the woman's just a decoy for her robber man who's hiding in the ditch. Pony tail, tennis shoes. Doesn't walk like a man in a wig masquerading as a woman. It's a woman. Can't hear her, but she's yelling. Waving her arms, walking backwards, facing me, inching off the shoulder into my lane.

It's a single driver. A man. Not another creep, I hope. Hey, mister. Please stop. Stop. I'm harmless, see? No guns. No knives. I don't want your drugs. Just a ride to town. Any town. A telephone. Maybe I could use your cell. Call somebody. Anybody. Please, mister. Slow down. Slow down.

It's not a busy highway this time of day. If I don't pick her up, who will? I could call 911 and report a stranded hitchhiker. Maybe she wouldn't like that. Don't have a schedule this morning. Could be an adventure picking her up. Hearing her tale of woe. But if it went sour . . .

Is he slowing, or is it my imagination? Honestly sir, I'm harmless. I'm in serious trouble. I'll repay you. Honest.

Man, she looks frantic. Maybe I stop and talk to her through the window. Maybe she opens her bag and pulls a gun. But she doesn't look like that.

I can see him sizing me up. Please, mister. I'm desperate.

She looks troubled, crazy. I could help her. But I could regret it too.

Please Lord, make him stop.

Oh, what the hell. I'd rather regret what I did than what I didn't do.

CAT TALE

Marvin slid an arm out of his shirt, loosened his belt, and let his pants fall to the floor. He shuffled to the easy chair and flopped into the molded contour of cushions. What a day. He edged the hassock closer with a heel, and lifted his feet, one at a time, into worn grooves of threadbare green frieze. His bare legs, hairless now, reminded him of highway maps with county roads in blue, interstates in red, and state parks in brown splotches. The troubled air he inhaled today escaped his lungs in a gravelly sigh. He closed his eyes. The telephone rang.

"Get that, will you, Tom?"

Tom sat under the table licking his paws.

"Never mind," Marvin said. "I'll get it."

"This is Betty at Maple Crest," a voice said. "Your wife has settled down and is sleeping. We'll keep an eye on her tonight and call you if her condition deteriorates. Now you get a good night's sleep yourself."

Marvin flopped back in the chair. Tom slicked himself until flickers of light reflected in his fur.

"I used to have black hair like that," Marvin said. He lifted his seed corn cap and combed fingers through sparc gray threads. "I'm afraid my tom-cattin' days are over. I'm afraid they've been over for a long time." He clasped his hands behind his head and closed his eyes. "I remember the last time we made love, Ella and me. It must have been ten, twelve years ago. Just about the time I thought I had transported her to heaven, she pops up with 'I think we oughta have a garage sale.'"

Tom looked up, extended a back leg, and polished it to the luster of glass.

"It looks like it'll be you and me, Tom. You did the right thing being born a cat. A new adventure every night. No heartbreak. No worry. No pain."

Tom stood, arched his back, and strode to the easy chair. As he walked between the chair and hassock, he brushed his back and tail against Marvin's legs, then sprang up on Marvin's chest.

Marvin stroked the sleek, black coat with one hand, then the other. He closed his eyes, the cat's weightless warmth filling the hollow of his chest. "Ella," he whispered.

Tom lifted a clawless paw to Marvin's lips.

"I'll let you out now, Tom." Marvin braced to stand. "Good night. But remember, no garage sales."

BEST BIRTHDAY WISHES

S*cene opens on an older couple driving on a deserted road. It is late evening, the scene lit by headlights and a bright moon. The man is driving, his wife listening to the radio in the passenger seat, half-asleep. Ahead, he spots a figure in the headlights.*

Pepper: What the hell. Do you see what I see?

Maude: *squinting.* I don't have my glasses on.

Pepper: Looks like a woman. Walks like a woman. Wonder what she's doing way out here this time of night?

> *He puts his foot on the brake.*

Maude: Just keep driving. Probably some tramp looking to make a few bucks.

Pepper: No car broken down along the road back there.

> *He taps the brakes again.*

Maude: Just keep going.

Pepper: Looks like she's all dolled up. Wow. Long dress. Are those shoes she's carrying? High heels?

Maude: Sure isn't a local. Just keep going.

Pepper: She might be stranded. Might have rolled her car and need help.

> *He brakes to a near stop.*

Maude: Might have stolen a car and run out of gas. Just keep going.

Pepper: We're miles from any farm. Ten miles to town. We at least have to offer help.

Maude: You've told me a million times. Don't stop for a hitchhiker.

Pepper: I'll just slow down a bit more. Roll down your window.

Maude: I'm not rolling down my damn window. Keep going. And for God's sake, speed up. She's swatting mosquitoes, not waving at you. She's not asking for your help.

Pepper: I'd feel bad if she got struck by a hit and run. Or got mauled by a bear.

THAT REMINDS ME

Maude: If she was a fat old hag, you wouldn't even notice her.

Pepper: Just crack your window a bit.

Maude groans and opens the window slightly.

Pepper: Hey, lady, need a . . .? Wow, did you see the look she gave me?

He speeds up.

Maude: I told you. Just keep driving. I've had enough bad luck today.

Pepper: Come on Maude, loosen up. It's my birthday. How much did you lose to your favorite slots tonight?

Maude: Not saying.

Pepper: Well, I won. $400. It only cost me $600. That might have been Lady Luck we just passed, walking out on me.

Maude: Dream on.

Pepper: Or walking in on me. Maybe we should turn around.

Maude: You're crazy, Pepper. Just keep going. I'm tired.

Pepper: I'll find some music on the radio. Something schmaltzy. Maybe put you in the mood.

Maude: Not likely.

Pepper: Maybe Lady Luck back there would like to give me a birthday present.

Maude: You wouldn't know what to do with it. A young woman like that would kill you.

Pepper: What a way to die.

Maude: I didn't tell you, Pepper, but I have a birthday present waiting for you at home.

She becomes animated and snuggles against him.

Pepper: What is it?

Maude: Surprise. Something you've never had before.

She puts her arm around his neck.

Pepper: Lord help me. Not tuberculosis, I hope.

Maude: The sooner you get home, the sooner you'll find out. Now get this buggy rolling. Happy birthday, you old codger.

MONEY

Charlie grabbed a handrail of the faux marble staircase of the old high school building, now a mini-mall of trendy shops and low budget offices. Young shoppers and young off-duty employees sped by him when he took a breather at the landing on the way down. Of course they were young. Everyone was younger than Charlie.

Why am I doing this? he asked himself again and again. *Why not stay home and sleep and watch reruns of* Mash *and play dominoes? Why not admit this is the final inning and, with such a lopsided score, there's no chance in hell of winning?*

Keep active, his doctor had counseled. *Exercise your body. Walk the stairs. Exercise your brain. Find volunteer work.* And that's what brought him to the mini-mall today, telephoning for donations to the local food shelf. "Your fifty-dollar gift will provide a Christmas dinner for a family of eight." He must have rattled that off a hundred times today. As if there were families of eight anymore.

At the foot of the stairs, he crowded against windowed walls of shops, steadied himself against kiosks and trash containers, and waited for a break in the pedestrian traffic before heading for the employee exit. He sniffed the aroma of hot caramel corn and, for a moment, considered buying a box. But why? It would stick in his teeth. And what had his dentist said about sweets?

At the door, he pulled on his Viking stocking cap and said goodnight to the guard, a chubby man in a black jacket, white shirt, and visored service hat that rode down to his ears. Charlie hadn't seen him before or didn't remember. The guard gave him a half-salute and a scanning glance.

"No pilfered merchandise on me," Charlie muttered. "Merry Christmas."

Snow crusted the steps on the landing outside. Charlie clung to the railing and scanned the parking lot. Pink-tinted lights reflected on falling snow, creating giant balls of cotton candy. At the curb, he crossed between two parked cars, their engines purring. One, a sleek BMW puffing an acrid diesel smell. The other, an old VW Beetle with a rowdy rap tune penetrating its snowy shell.

Another pain-in-the-ass day. Christmas, but no one in the Christmas spirit. He should have known. The whole Christmas season had started bad, ugly bad. An argument with his wife Jen over finances. Or the lack thereof. She wanted control of the checking account. Fine. Weeks later, he picked up the mail when she was shopping. Two overdraft notices. Two. He hoped she'd bring it up over dinner. She didn't.

This morning before leaving for the mini-mall, Charlie held his mug out. "How are we doing on the checking account?"

Jen rose and poured coffee. "Okay, I guess."

"We got two overdraft notices from the bank. What's our balance?"

"Oh, I meant to remind you to make a deposit. Didn't I mention that?"

"What's the balance? Where's the checkbook?"

"I haven't balanced it lately. Don't make a big deal of it. Just make a deposit." She leaned one hand on the table, the other on her hip. "You make it sound like it's my fault you can't support us."

"When I get home tonight, we'll straighten this out. And I'll manage the checkbook." Charlie clanked his mug on the table. "It's snowing. I'll take the bus this morning." He rose and grabbed his coat and gloves from the closet and pulled the stocking cap over his ears.

"You look like a fool," his wife said.

Now he was walking through the parking lot, a large lot shared with the adjacent strip mall. The snow-covered cars all looked alike. He hadn't remembered to note his lot location, unsure even which lot he had parked in. He rethought the morning, and all that surfaced was the checkbook argument.

"Damned woman," he muttered. "Thinks that as long as there are blank checks in the book, there's funds to cover them." That was fine when he hauled in the big salary and the commission checks and the hefty annual bonuses. Now it was the dreadful fixed income of social security and his retirement check. And an investment portfolio so paltry he wouldn't discuss it.

76

Dinnertime darkness and foul weather thinned the parking lot fast. He dodged a car that hadn't been swept, the wipers spewing snow right and left. He jumped when a car he leaned on popped into reverse and backed toward him.

We'll make this a process of elimination, Charlie thought, *if I survive. Start at row one and look for the boxy SUV. No help that it's red; all vehicles are white tonight.*

He picked his way up rows one and two, down three and four. Nothing. Snow fell heavier, or was it wind? Tough to see. He trudged on. Up rows five and six, down rows seven and eight. He pulled the cap down to his eyes and snugged his jacket collar. Where was that damned car? A different lot? Behind the mini-mall where employees were supposed to park? He stood in the shelter of the building wall, scanning the lot, angered over his failing memory, wanting to quit something—this piddling volunteer work? This challenging winter driving? This purpose-less life? He walked to the stairs of the employee entrance.

Inside, Charlie pulled off his stocking cap and shook snow against his leg.

"Problem?" the guard asked. "Car wouldn't start?"

"Can't find the damn thing." Charlie brushed snow off his jacket, pulled off his gloves, and wrung his icy hands. "They all look alike."

"You have one of those key doodads that flash your parking lights when you hit *unlock*?" the guard asked. "I'll call the office and have somebody look with you."

Charlie reached into his pants pocket. No keys. Jacket pocket. None. He patted his pants, front and back. Nothing. "Oh shit," he said. "I took the bus this morning."

"Wait a minute," the guard said. "A woman came in here a half hour ago looking for a man in a Viking stocking cap. Your wife maybe?"

"Could have been, but I doubt it."

"She said she waited outside, but might have missed you with all the snow and everything. She figured you took the bus home."

Charlie stared at the guard. Of course, the BMW outside. That was her car. He pulled his cap back on. "Then I guess the bus is what I'll take."

THAT REMINDS ME

"Strange day today," Jen said as she set a platter of roast beef on the table. Charlie wrapped his still-numb fingers in a napkin and inhaled the steam rising from the gravy boat. He noticed Jen wore a dress tonight, a dress she wore on their honeymoon. Pearls, too. Lipstick, hair.

"My daughter called. She sounded strangely determined. Confident. She said her daughter and DeShawn were not getting married. And they were not having children. Definitely not having children. Anatomically impossible. I was dumbstruck. And then she snapped, 'Sorry to dash your hopes for great grandchildren, Jennifer.'"

"DeShawn? Who's DeShawn? Her current live-in?"

"Oh, you didn't know? They've been living together since May. Wonderful young man. I met him a few times. He sells cars for a big dealer."

"Why haven't I met him?"

"She didn't know how you'd respond to his . . . his ethnicity."

"Oh, for Christ's sake." Charlie dropped his fork and knife. "That girl drives me crazy."

"You'd feel different if she were your granddaughter."

"No, I wouldn't."

"Anyway," Jen continued, "I got to thinking. No big wedding. No need to budget for one. Between you and me, I've been stashing away a few hundred here and there. That's what wedding planners advise, you know. Plan for it, budget for it, save for it."

"Wait, a minute," Charlie said. "Where's her dad?"

"Good question."

Charlie retrieved his knife and fork. "Does that explain the overdrafts?"

"Partially. I met with the banker this afternoon. We closed the wedding savings account. And I cashed a couple old CDs. We're solvent again." She handed him the platter of roast beef. "Does that make you happy?"

Charlie helped himself and handed the platter back. She passed him his favorite corn casserole and smiled. "And you can have the checkbook back."

Charlie's shoulders drooped. He leaned back in his chair holding the warm casserole and wiped his mouth with a napkin.

"And how was your day?" she asked.

LITTLE WOMEN

My daughter's scolding echoes over and over. *Stupid. Disgusting.* Funny—the kids were taught to honor thy father and thy mother, and be true to their feelings. Can't do both. Maybe it is stupid. Maybe it looks disgusting. But my feelings are real. They're sincere.

The wife's therapist at Good Shepherd says walking is the cure for whatever ails you—stress, boredom, weight gain. Maybe a walk along the frozen edge of the river will reduce the stress. Maybe not. It's worth a try.

A feisty wind is blowing from the east, a harbinger of change in these parts. Change is good. Change is welcome.

It should feel cold, but it doesn't. Nothing feels. Hands are warm in these chopper mitts. Feet in Sorel boots. Head in the Elmer Fudd hat that always draws a laugh. Stinging fingers would be welcome, proof there's life in this body.

What time is it? About five. Vera will be rolling her chair to the dining hall at Good Shepherd soon. She won't eat. She won't, unless someone's there to coax her. Someone in the family. But no one's there, so she won't eat. It's not too late for me to drive in, but the doctor said no night driving, no driving when you're stressed, no driving if you're tired. Three reasons not to go.

It's quiet out here. Peaceful. No sound except the crunch of snow underfoot. Owls will hoot soon, Popeye and Olive Owl, my regular visitors along the river all winter. Might hear the drumbeat of a pileated woodpecker. Might hear a crow or blue jay squawk and scold, like the kids. Might hear east wind whisper through the white pines, whisper accusations and nod to each other in agreement. *Stupid. Disgusting.*

Vera. My little sparrow. Five-foot nothing. A hundred pounds and shrinking. Not much left to love. So what now? Is sex drive supposed to disappear when you're left alone? The kids think so. In her day, Vera was all this man could handle. Tiny, almost miniature, needy in a good way. Irresistible, like a puppy you must hold and squeeze and press against your body and feel the warmth, the softness.

Now she's at Good Shepherd.

There are others. There's Colette, my little chickadee, at the Super Market. Small again. Sensuous and small. Looking like she needs someone to protect her, to shield her. It must have seemed obvious when my grocery shopping became a daily routine, always checking-out in her lane, making small talk, taking a risk with my suggestive chatting.

And Penny the hairdresser. Penny, my little canary. Also small and vulnerable. It's more than a lonely man can handle when she wraps her arms around your neck with the cape and presses against you. Then bends you backwards into the sink to massage your scalp. And, oh my God, when she blows loose hairs off your neck. Shivers. She deserves a hug, what with raising that toddler alone and trying to make ends meet. She got suspicious when my appointments went from six weeks to five to four. Maybe it wasn't smart to offer her the fifty dollars. But it could have been a loan. It sure wasn't smart to mention it to my kids. That prompted them to call her and ask what was going on. What was going on? Nothing. Or almost nothing. But the hug was worth it. The full body hug around that tiny waist. She didn't hug back, but she didn't pull away either.

The kids say, *Stay away. Stay home. Feed your birds. Your nuthatches and finches depend on you.* What do they know about a man's needs? *Stay home and play solitaire,* they say. Don't they know solitaire gets boring after a hundred games? Depressing after a thousand? Fatal after a million?

That's Popeye hooting from the other side of the river. Stop. Listen for Olive's answer. This might be a good place to rest, get off the river, and find a stump to sit on. The trees are tall along the shore here, tall, straight, uniform. The one that bends and wears a foot of snow on its horizontal trunk catches the eye. Isn't that the way it goes? The old timer, the bent guy, gets the attention. May as well keep walking.

There's deer tracks and rabbit tracks and fox tracks, all kinds of tracks. Fun to follow them into the woods and see where they lead. Maybe keep on walking, walk deeper into the woods. Maybe get lost when it gets dark. Maybe have a heart attack and not be found until spring. Maybe not be missed until spring. Maybe that's what they want. *Would serve him right,* they'd say. Better to stay on the river. There's open water ahead where the river shallows.

Hear that rippling sound? That's the rapids, the shallow stretch. It's dark against the white snow. Strange how fast night sets in. There's a pale sliver of moon up there. See if there's a spot where the moon reflects on open water.

Remember last summer when you first saw Penny the hairdresser? Sitting on the beach, nursing her baby, trilling a lullaby? Sand as white as snow, the lake behind her rippling like the river is now, the sun reflecting a trail of gold. Remember the glow of her skin, her pale, angel skin, the sun creating a halo around her trailing blond hair? Penny, my little canary.

The wind's coming up now, shifting to the north. Pines that whispered before shout now, a rushing sound like a freight train. It's wind screaming the old refrain, but with gusto. *Stupid. Disgusting.*

A flock of small birds scrambles in loose formation from downriver, finches returning after a day at the feeder. Must be a hundred of them, scrambling, chirping, chatting. Goldfinches, though not gold now. But when late winter sun hits them, the gold returns. They can change their colors. Maybe there's hope. But they'll change back again next year, so what's the point?

I'm getting tired. Trudging through snow, breaking trail, heading nowhere. Wishing for an epiphany, a vision, a clue. Nothing. The old birch tree ahead bends down to touch the snow. Must have uprooted in last summer's wind. Good place to rest.

Something flying up there, something big. Could be an eagle. It is. He's circling. What does he see? Dead meat? Dead man?

Maybe it's a sign. Eagles are medicine birds with magic powers. Good stuff. He's king. He's spirit and balance and courage in battle. He's a guiding beacon. Might be the reincarnation of a forefather who cares, who understands, who says accept yourself the way you are and to hell with what other people think.

He's circling slower, circling lower, lower. He lifts now and heads downriver, heading toward home, screeching *follow me, follow me.*

Yes, wait, I'll follow. Yes, wait.

SUNDAY MORNING

Five after seven and Fred's still in the barn. Going to be tight getting to mass by eight. He'll have to shower and eat something, and it's a half-hour drive to church. So we'll be late again, sneaking in when the priest faces the altar, I hope, and finding a couple empty seats in the back. Or climbing the rickety choir steps and being stared at by the ladies in hats trying to carry a tune.

What in God's name was that? Sounded like a shotgun. Fred must be shooting pigeons again. Or one of Elmer's feral cats. I wish he'd hurry. I got his eggs in the fry pan and bread in the toaster. Maybe time for me to have another cup of coffee. Wish I could help with chores, but he says I make the cows nervous. Cuts down on their milk production, and Lord knows we need all the production we can get. A month behind on the mortgage. Two or three months behind on the feed bill. Don't dare answer the phone anymore. Seems it's always somebody looking to get paid.

Not to mention the leaky roof. The well that's slowing to a dribble. The buildings that haven't been painted since Dad willed us the farm. There must be something to be thankful for. Apples setting on the trees by the ton. Chickens laying. Suzanne graduating at the top of her class.

And she'll need tuition money in September. Where will I come up with that? Don't know, but I'll figure it out. More than anything, I want her to get that education, learn a trade, break out of the world I've suffered through. Sometimes I wish she'd been born a boy and had an interest in farming. Could be helping Fred now.

Got to remember to bring the offertory envelope. Hope whoever counts it doesn't laugh when they see it's only a dollar. The milk check won't get here 'til Friday. Should tell Fred about my lumps, maybe see a doctor and have a check-up. And Fred should get serious about those stomach cramps. Probably ulcers. He's earned them.

THAT REMINDS ME

Doesn't talk about them much. Just grabs his stomach now and then and bends over. Looks like he's in real pain.

Actually doesn't talk much about anything. Not since his prize Holstein broke through the fence and bloated in the cornfield. Blamed himself for not digging new fence posts. Went into kind of a depression. Hasn't come out yet. Doesn't go fishing on Sunday afternoons anymore. Doesn't want to play pinochle with Elmer and Marge. Day after day, just chores, field work, chores, sleep. Well, kind of sleep. Mostly toss and turn.

I could gas up the old Ford pickup, but Fred wouldn't like that. Man's job, he says. C'mon, Fred. Hurry up, damn it.

Sorry, Lord.

Canning factory is hiring. Could get a job there. Make a few bucks and spend most of it paying for rides back and forth. And who would make Fred's dinner? Or run to town for parts? Could sell tomatoes and potatoes and cucumbers out of the garden in a couple weeks. But everybody will have more than they can eat out of their own gardens.

Ah, this heat. Sweating like a hog. Dress sticks to me. Can't stand in front of the fan all day. The radio says no relief in sight. And no rain. Corn's starting to wither and yellow. Second crop hay is only ankle high. Might end up having to buy feed this winter. One more thing.

I don't know what the answer is. Sometimes I wonder if it's all worth it. That's what Fred said this morning when he went out to do chores. Is it all worth it?

DAMAGED GOODS

"She wants the house. She wants the kids. She wants my pension. What do I get? Credit card bills. And her dog." Larry and Jack sit stools apart at the bar of the Broken Hart, Larry lamenting his recent divorce settlement.

"I should have known it was coming," Larry continues. "She's been threatening for years. But you know, it's like a death in the family. It's inevitable, but it's a shock when it happens."

Jack sees Larry's reflection in the mirror behind the bar. He lowers his head and watches through his eyebrows to avert Larry's gaze, to avoid getting sucked into Larry's mumbling monologue.

Avis wipes the counter, checks the thermometer, and adjusts the thermostat. Muggy summer air seeps through withered window frames and beneath the skewed front door. A rain squall makes its way through town, darkening the sky to an early nightfall.

"What did I do to deserve this?" Larry swivels the beer bottle. "I asked her that, and she couldn't answer. Couldn't come up with one good reason. Not one huge thing, she said, but little things. Like forgetting her birthday. Slamming the car door. Licking the butter knife."

Avis leans on the bar in front of Larry, her scooped T-shirt revealing a field of freckles. "And what have you done to make her toes wiggle? Nothing. Want another Bud?"

Larry scowls, his jaw drops.

Jack finishes his drink. "Gotta run, Avis. This marriage counseling is too close to home. See you next time."

Rain skids off to the north, and an afternoon sun wrestles through wisps of charcoal clouds. Steam undulates above the roadway. A faint rainbow emerges and frames the landscape in surreal peace and serenity. Jack chuckles to himself. The pot at the end of the rainbow holds something other than gold.

He walks to his car. Drive home? But why? Larry's maudlin whining in the bar resonates with him. He sits in the car, uncertain and alienated. What's waiting for him at home? Boredom. Anxiety. Pain. What mood will she be in? And why should her mood determine his? But it does.

A glint of sun glares through the windshield. The breeze stiffens into wind that tumbles renegade leaves down the street. A beer can somersaults in their wake. Jack slides his sunglasses on and leaves the parking lot. He tunes in a country western radio station where a cowboy wails about love lost. Sounds familiar.

A couple miles out of town, a black SUV is nosed in the ditch, half-buried in weeds and brush, smashed into a massive oak trunk. Jack slams the brakes and bolts from his car. Steam whistles from the SUV's radiator. He smells gasoline and hears the engine chugging.

The driver is in the car, slumped over the steering wheel. Jack opens the door, turns the ignition key off. He lifts the driver out and drags him to the roadway. A middle-aged man, Jack's age, dressed as if driving home from an office job. Unconscious. Jack calls 911 on his cell phone. He checks for breathing. The man stirs. He blinks an eye. Jack kneels beside him, fingers on his wrist. The radiator whistles, and gasoline reeks through rain-freshened air, mixed with the odor of trampled weeds. "What happened?" he whimpers.

"It's okay. Paramedics are on the way."

"Where's my car?"

"It's here. In the ditch. You drove off the road. You'll be okay."

Jack loosens the man's tie and opens his collar. He checks for bleeding, notes a nasty bruise on the forehead, but sparse blood. Knuckles red and bleeding.

"I dozed off," the man whispers. Then, "Cell phone. Jacket pocket."

Jack lifts his sport coat lapel and reaches for the cell phone. "Okay, I have it."

"Keep it. Destroy it."

"I can't do that. And nothing's going to happen to you."

"Keep it."

"I'll give it to the paramedics."

"Keep it. Destroy it." He swings his arms in circles, twists his body.

"Okay, I'll keep it. Now relax, please." He checks for circulation. Irregular pulse. He glances at his watch. Five-thirty. "Do you want me to call someone? Your wife?"

"God, no."

Jack talks encouragement to him, asks him what state he lives in, who's President, what is the month, the year, anything to keep him conscious.

"Not going to make it." The man relaxes in Jack's arms. He struggles. His eyes roll upward and close. "Tell her I'm sorry."

"Hang in there, buddy," Jack says. "Hang in there." He holds the man's hand, feels a slight squeeze, then relaxed, limp. From a distance, a siren wails.

Back in his car, Jack sits, uncertain where to go. He returns to the Broken Hart, too unsettled for home. A few pickup trucks are nosed into the concrete ramp in front. He opens the door of the bar. Humidity and rain release the sultry aroma of beer-soaked bar counters and smoke-drenched walls.

"Back already?" Avis asks.

Jack sits at his former stool. Larry has left. Locals shake dice at the far end of the bar. Avis hands him a Bud.

He hears the faint sound of a tune coming from his pocket. The cell phone. He retrieves it, stares, holds it, uncertain what to do. A frightened wife wondering why her husband's late? Kids wanting a ride home from the pool?

"Answer it," Avis says.

It quits ringing. "You're not going to believe this," he says, and tells Avis about the accident.

"You'd better check the message. Might be a lady in distress."

"I can't."

"Here, I'll do it." Avis reaches for the cell phone and plays the message.

Hey, cowboy. What a ride. Counting the hours 'til Friday. And in a giddy voice, *Tata.*

Avis scowls at the phone. "That didn't sound like a wife to me. Damn men. Can't be happy with one woman. And now he's on the way to the hospital. Or the morgue. I won't say it serves him right, but it serves him right."

THAT REMINDS ME

"Don't jump to conclusions."

"You know I'm right. I've had enough relationships to know that there's no such thing as a match made in heaven. You gotta work with what you got." She pauses and looks at Jack. "You might think about that yourself." She hustles down the bar to the locals.

Jack's chest tightens, feeling more yearning than guilt. He needs a soft shoulder to touch. Silky hair to bury his face in. A sunset to share. A rainbow. *Tell her I'm sorry*, echoes in his ears. *Tell her I'm sorry.*

He leaves the Broken Hart and walks to his car. He calls home and hears the answering machine message. She's not home, or not answering the phone. "Hey, Honey," he says. "I'm on my way home."

GAME THEORY

Back in the seventies, a pestering tension prevailed, an inkling that America teetered on the brink of revolution. We had survived Watergate and the flower-powered hippie movement. The war in Viet Nam inched toward a hollow, bitter stalemate. Computers promised to make our Buck Rogers dreams come true.

Main Street America wasn't exempt. The national scene hovered like smog over the heartlands and tempted innocents to join a foray they knew nothing about. Time-honored customs and standards of conduct were challenged, and the elders failed to meet the challengers. Customs and standards fell like flies.

Being a teenager in Browns Prairie complicated Ben's life. How much of his rebellion was hormonal? After all, it was spring. How much of his turmoil was business as usual?

Browns Prairie was a one-stoplight town with the prescribed array of residences, stores, churches, schools. Neighbors read of riots in Watts and Nixon's resignation in the face of impeachment, yet felt separated from it all. At the same time, they felt an attraction, stopping to watch a televised neighborhood on fire in L.A. or presidential cabinet firing in Washington. They felt an urge to be part of it, like watching a ball game from the stands and wanting to jump on the field.

Watching from the sidelines was easy for Ben. This was his last year in high school, and the prospect of attending college in the fall was daunting. He didn't play sports, he wasn't academically inclined, and he didn't have close friends.

Not that his home life was better. Dad drank too much, Mom prayed too much, and his young sister was such an easy target there was no satisfaction tormenting her. Dad nagged him about his weight. "You oughta be a linebacker, boy," he'd say, working the dials on the Zenith TV. Hopeful Mom bought a football at the Thrift Store, and it sat on his bookshelf until he left home.

Ben's neighbor Helen Brockett was cut from the same cloth: a loner, lackluster student who lived with her mother in a broken home, as it was then called. Although Ben and Helen walked to school together, it was out of coincidence, not intention. They were not friends. Confidantes or sounding boards, maybe. But not friends.

If Ben was fat, Helen was skinny. String Bean Brockett. She wore a man-sized watch/stopwatch that told time in four time zones. She owned an electronic calculator, the first in the neighborhood, but wasn't allowed to bring it to school.

Nerdy Helen waited in the public library for her mother to return from work at Good Shepherd Assisted Living. She despised school and spent classroom time avoiding teachers, and lunch hour avoiding classmates. That was her saving grace for Ben; she was more shunned and more disliked than he.

Back in the seventies, Woolworth's Five and Dime sold small pets in the rear of the store. Goldfish, parakeets, and half-dollar sized turtles with designs painted on their backs. Ben's dad prohibited pets. "If you had to milk cows twice a day, and chase pigs out of the garden, and stay up all night lambing, you'd hate critters too," he'd rant.

Out of want of companionship at any level, or to test the waters of adolescent rebellion, Ben bought a turtle. It lived in his pocket the first day until Ben found a secluded spot behind the garage for a shoebox home. The challenge was not to keep the secret from his family; it was to find someone trustworthy to share it with. There was no one, except Helen. Ben told her about Jimi Turtle.

"How do you know it's a Jimi?" she asked. "Maybe it's a Janis." She turned it over. Ben reached for it, and she swung her arm around. Ben was embarrassed. His family didn't talk about sex. He didn't talk about it in health class. "I think you're right. See?" She pointed with her ballpoint pen.

"Give him back," Ben said.

Days later, Helen asked if she could borrow Jimi for an overnight visit. "There's an old aquarium in my basement. If he likes it there, I'll buy one too."

Helen missed school the next day, and the next. When Ben saw her, she said Jimi ran away.

"Ran away," Ben said. "What do you mean *ran away*?"

"He ran away," she said.

"You mean you killed him."

"He ran away."

Death was on Ben's mind. Tragic death. A local, Private Tucker Roth, was killed in action. Killed. Dead. That should have made Jimi's death insignificant, but didn't.

Immediately, the County Chapter of the Democratic Party enjoined the local Daughters of Martha to stage a protest parade down Main Street, concluding at City Hall. They brought bullhorns and banners, improvised anti-government slogans, whipped up a frenzy of protest for the press.

The following Saturday, a warm spring day, a crowd congregated at Our Savior's—idealistic students, unemployed middle-agers, disaffected seniors with time on their hands, a second-rate hodgepodge of folks with no common goal or clear purpose. They shouted "Hell no, we won't go," within the shadow of the tabernacle to the chagrin of the Daughters of Martha.

Helen and Ben watched the assembly from the shadows of the bandstand across from the church parking lot. Helen broke the silence. "And to think I saw it on Mulberry Street." She laughed. She placed her hand on Ben's as it rested on the railing. "I'm sorry about Jimi," she said.

He feigned not hearing her and pointed to a person being interviewed by the press. "Isn't that Mrs. Roth?" It was quiet again.

"I'm leaving here the day I graduate," Helen said. "Gonna join the Army."

It was her first indication of compassion, her first confidence shared, their first clumsy moment.

Helen delivered on her promise. She left for army basic training the Monday after high school graduation, took advanced courses in computer programming, and tested her way into MIT after discharge. She graduated with honors and landed a job with IBM where, in her spare time, she designed computer games. Her clever games caught the attention of a startup company in Silicon Valley who hired her away with a massive stock option. All this news over the years from her mother to Ben's mother across the back fence.

For the high school fifteen-year reunion, millionaire Helen came home to rescue her mother from Browns Prairie and take her to their new home in a gated community overlooking the Pacific. She was attractive in her tall black slacks, her black turtleneck, her hair in an un-Browns Prairie casual cut. Ben saw her at the wine bar. "Pardon me, but you look like someone I knew in an earlier life."

Helen smiled. "That line is so Midwestern. It would never cut it on the coast."

"It worked for me here in Browns Prairie." Ben flashed a wedding ring. "We'll miss your mom. She kept us current on your wild and crazy journey. Congratulations."

"I want you to know the first game I designed was called Jimi's Journey," she said. "The trick was to help this little turtle find his way out of the house, out of town, out to the ocean. It worked."

FRAGRANCE

An elfin Korean waitress darts toward the couple seated on bar stools. She wears an alluring fragrance which the man finds provocative, like fresh citrus.

"Hi. I'm Kim," the waitress says. "Something from the bar?"

"Miller Lite. And Merlot for the lady," he says.

"Change that. Jack Daniels on the rocks," she says, "and Miller Lite for the gentleman."

He eyes the waitress as she leaves, then turns. "That's a switch."

"A woman's prerogative." She sits erect and speaks to her hands folded before her.

"I feel overdressed," she says.

"You look great." He opens the menu, scans it, and sets it down.

"The beret. Over the top?"

"Perfect." He glances at his watch.

She looks out the window. "Kate and Bob are splitting. Can't believe they've paid for the wedding yet."

"How does Bob feel about that?" He folds his napkin into geometric designs.

"Kate hasn't told him."

He opens his cell phone, listens, taps a number, then places the phone on the table.

The drinks arrive. She lifts her glass in a toast, then hesitates. "Happy Anniversary."

He snaps his head toward her, then toward the calendar on his phone. "And they said it wouldn't last. Twelve years. It seems like yesterday."

"Thirteen," she says. "It may seem like yesterday, but it's today."

She closes her eyes and drifts. The alluring fragrance, the provocative, deceptive fragrance is sea air. She's strolling the promenade deck of a cruise ship, clinging to a tanned stranger she doesn't remember meeting.

THAT REMINDS ME

JOANNA

Joanna sits in her modest Minneapolis home as a blanket of fog coaxes an early February darkness. Through her living room window, a pale globe of streetlight illuminates the corner intersection. No need to pull shades or draw drapes. The room is dark. No one will see her.

On the street, headlights appear through the fog, approach, and cast shadows that rotate around the walls. How that fascinated her as a child when Mother and Dad bought this house sixty years ago.

She should warm a bowl of soup, make toast, drink tea, but she's not hungry. She feels a cough building and slides a Kleenex from her sleeve. She coughs, then presses her chest and inhales deep breaths to relax her muscles. Her church lady friend guessed pneumonia. "Where would I get that?" Joanna responded. "I only get outside once a week and that's to mass."

Her hands fall to her lap. She tightens the afghan around her legs and fingers the herringbone stitches, the gold and brown and orange yarns recognizable in remnants of light. Mother crocheted this. She sat in this chair, much as Joanna sits now, waiting, waiting, until she couldn't sit. Then she lay in bed, waiting, waiting.

Where had the years gone? Dad dying on his seventy-eighth birthday in the front bedroom twelve years ago. Mother moving into Joanna's room until she died two years later. And John. How long has he been dead? Four or five years. Poor John. What a disaster.

The streetlight glows brighter now; the fog looks like snow, almost Christmas-y. It reminds her of Albert. Albert with the slick black hair and gap between his front teeth. The weightlifter who worked with her at S&L Department Store, she selling everyday dresses, he back in the stockroom wearing a white shirt and tie, bucking for a job in sales.

Her co-workers hinted that Albert had inquired about her. Next thing she knew he asked her to a movie at Radio City. The red ticket stub is still tucked in the frame of her vanity mirror.

After the movie, he drove her back northeast to Nye's. Joanna hadn't been in a nightclub before, hadn't been in anything grander than a 3.2 beer joint. She was dumbstruck when she saw the lipstick-red leather booths and jeweled light fixtures dangling from the ceiling. The long bar that extended to the rear of the building, the mirrored backdrop, the hundreds, the thousands of bottles.

Albert nudged her. "Cool, huh?"

Joanna gaped when Albert called the piano player by name. "Evening, Lou," he said.

"Evening yourself, Albert," she replied. "Who's the young lady? You trying to make me jealous?"

Joanna and Albert dated twice after that and ended at Nye's Piano Bar each night. At Christmas, he asked her to view the holiday decorations downtown.

He held Joanna's mittened hand as they walked along Nicollet Avenue watching the animated Christmas display windows. Dayton's theme was nursery rhymes—Jack and Jill climbing the hill, Little Miss Muffett sitting on her tuffet, Little Boy Blue blowing his horn.

"Cool," said Albert. "Downright cool."

A bus pulled to the curb, its exhaust stinking acrid fumes. From its doors, struggling kids tugged excited parents. "Look at Red Riding Hood, Mom. Look at the big, bad wolf." Somewhere above the awnings, a loud speaker blared "Silver Bells."

Someday, these could be my kids, Joanna thought. *Someday they could be ours.*

Albert slipped his arm around her waist at the corner and placed his lips against the babushka that covered her ears. "I love you," he whispered.

Joanna struggles to remember what happened next. She remembers sitting at the piano bar at Nye's, Lou and Albert harmonizing on "Baby, It's Cold Outside."

"Join in," Lou called. Joanna dropped her eyes, shook her head, and stirred her Shirley Temple. Albert wrapped his arms around her and faked a shiver. "Baby, it's cool outside."

"I have something to ask you," Albert said when he finished his drink. "Let's go where we have some privacy."

Joanna lifts herself in the chair to wrap the afghan around her shoulders. She has replayed this memory a million times. How they walked upstairs to Albert's apartment. How he turned on a small table lamp and pulled the shades. How he lit a cigarette and offered one to her. Good Lord, she wouldn't smoke a cigarette. How he reached into a cabinet for a bottle of whiskey and offered her a drink. For Heaven's sake, she hadn't finished her Shirley Temple at Nye's. How he stacked a handful of 45s on the record player and motioned her to sit beside him. How he flicked off the light and wrapped his arm around her. How the rosy glow of his cigarette lit his face when he inhaled. How she was nervous and excited and afraid. How he snuffed out the cigarette, took a long drink of whiskey, and turned to face her. One hand held her shoulder, the other slid down her back to her waist, then up inside her sweater.

What happened then? She must have screamed. She must have struggled to break free. She must have stumbled to the door, patting the wall for a light switch, wondering where he had hung her coat. And when she found the light and her coat, she avoided looking at him. She heard his laugh, first a titter, then a hearty guffaw. "Nobody runs out on Cool Albert, Baby," he yelled. "Nobody."

She unlocked the door and ran down the stairs.

Albert called early the next morning and didn't wait for Joanna to say hello. "I'm sorry, Baby. I'm sorry for how I acted last night."

Joanna was stunned. Albert apologizing? Cool Albert apologizing?

"Please forgive me. Please." Pause, and then, "Are you there, Joanna?"

Joanna felt her anger lift, felt a smile creep across her lips. She tossed away her thoughts of regret and opened her mouth to speak.

"Joanna. Are you there, Joanna? Joanna?"

Days later, when her mother asked what happened to the *nice young man*, Joanna related the skimpiest of details. Mother drew her own conclusion and must have shared the story with Joanna's father. "What did you expect, girl?" he said. "You think the guy's gonna buy a pig in a poke?"

Joanna stares at the streetlight, now a warm yellow glow. The furnace fan kicks on, and she shivers. *Tired makes me cold*, she thinks.

Hungry makes me cold. Another cough creeps up her throat, and she reaches for a Kleenex. A siren wails in the distance, a police car or an ambulance or a firetruck. Bad news for somebody.

Ambient light in the room reveals a clutter of containers along the floor. Boxes, stuffed shopping bags, wastebaskets, more boxes, more bags, a hamper. A narrow path connects the kitchen to the living room where she sits, to the bathroom, to the bedroom. She has kicked boxes as she navigates the path to straighten it, only to find she must sidle like a crab, shifting weight from heavy hip to heavy hip, arms extended for balance.

Reliving the Albert experience tires her, as it has tired her for years. *What if?* she wondered years ago. *What if?* she wonders now. Might it have been so bad? He said, "I love you." He said he had something to ask me, something in private. I might have relaxed for a moment, forgot the nuns' harping about avoiding the occasions of sin. If only . . . if only . . .

She looks at the cluttered room. She has no will to clean, no desire, no energy. Embarrassing. Admit it, she doesn't know how to clean. Doesn't want any help cleaning. Mother will clean. At least Mother would clean if she was alive. Since then, the Cool Whip containers, the cottage cheese containers, the yogurt cups accumulate by the bags full. Stacks of unread shopper newspapers guard the door. Recycling bins in the kitchen—plastic, glass, tin—overflow and mingle on the floor. When Mother died, Joanna changed locks on the doors and kept the keys. Nosy family members and neighbors need not bother. If they visit, they can stand on the front stoop.

Joanna relaxes in her chair and closes her eyes. Coughing has weakened her, made her faint and dizzy. An image of John flashes before her. John, her second regret, spoiled and helpless after living with his doting mother all his life. *Maybe we had something in common,* she muses. Something, but not enough to forge a relationship. John had a job, drove a Pontiac Chieftain, drank in moderation. But how could she not compare him to Albert? And when she did, John was plain vanilla; Albert was Neapolitan. Cool Neapolitan.

John had dropped a hint about getting married. "Think of the money we'd save. One house to maintain instead of two. One insurance policy. One property tax bill."

Joanna had met John's mother, a crotchety old woman with

white hair pulled back in a severe bun, black-rimmed glasses over squinty eyes, a metal cane she swung at everything, everyone in her way. Spoke only to John, and that was in Polish.

"Have you talked to your mother about that?" Joanna asked. "She might not like another woman in the house."

John laughed. "Just kidding," he said. "Just trying to make a joke."

Joanna should rise from this chair. Open a can of soup. Get some nourishment. She places her hands on the side arms and lifts. Nothing. She feels weak, dizzy, nauseous. Another coughing spell begins its tickling journey. This is a bad one. This one will hurt. Maybe she should call the ambulance. What good would that do? They couldn't get in the house.

The cough erupts with explosive force. She feels pressure on her eyeballs. Her head splits. Her lungs burn. She holds her chin to steady it. Her eyes tear. Her nose runs. She leans forward while the cough wracks her body.

Stooped with her head between her knees, she opens her eyes to a bag of Cool Whip containers at her feet. Even in ambient light, the dark letters of the logo glare against the white background. She stares until her eyes focus on the word *Cool*. Cool. Cool. Cool Albert.

A strong hand slides up and down her back.

Her grimace softens. Yes, Albert. Yes, yes.

HAPPY HOUR

"Dad, you'll never guess who I saw yesterday. Your old neighbor Lyle Sutton. Lyle, with a woman, no less." Craig Barnes steadied his father as he rose from the car seat in the Arboretum parking lot. Afternoon sun sparkled through leaves at the slightest breeze. A squirrel scolded from a park bench.

"Lyle with a woman? That's hard to believe." Mr. Barnes snugged his tweedy flat cap and zipped his jacket, then reached in the car for his walking stick.

"He introduced me. Catherine something." Craig reached for his father's arm. "Met her on a senior dating site."

"Why that cagey old fox. Good for him, I guess. How long has he been widowed? Ten, twelve years?"

"Same as you, Dad. Remember? He seemed happy, eager for me to meet her. Invited me to sit and chat. He asked about you. Said I should mention the dating site to you."

They walked the park paths, through chrysanthemum gardens and hosta beds—their autumn Saturday afternoon ritual. Oaks held their leaves in steadfast green. Basswood hinted at lime and yellow. Birch trees were gold, and leaves tumbled like butterflies in the breeze.

"Would you like to try, Dad? I'll help you."

"Try what?" Mr. Barnes tried to suppress a smile.

"On-line dating."

"No, Craig. No."

"What do you have to lose?"

"My pride. My dignity. My IRAs if she's a swindler. Besides that, what do I have to gain?"

"Winter's coming. Wouldn't you like to snuggle with a good woman? I'll work on your profile tonight."

"I can hear your mother laughing, shaking her head in disbelief."

"I can hear her laughing too, and yelling *Go for it.*"

THAT REMINDS ME

At Cranberry Pines Country Club, the bartender polished glasses, lifting them, watching neon light refract like stars. "Early for you, isn't it, Craig? Looking for the Happy Hour specials?" The bartender stopped, slapped a cardboard coaster on the bar, and placed the usual tap beer in front of him.

"My dad's having dinner in the restaurant." He pointed through the latticework divider. "A lady he met on the internet. I'm watching him in the mirror, that table by the window."

"Watching him? What's to watch?"

"You know the kind of people those dating sites attract. Perverts, psychotics, con artists, all preying on the unsuspecting."

"You're watching too much television."

"I've developed a lexicon for definitions women use online. 'Loves to travel' means a trip to Rochester once a year. 'Adventurous' means willing to sample every dish at the Chinese Buffet. 'Voracious reader' means she reads both Ann Landers and the comics. And 'hair color.' There should be a new category called dyed-blond-natural-brown-gray roots." He sipped his beer. "It's a liar's paradise."

A fortyish woman sat at the bar a few stools down, her elbows resting on the star-flecked countertop. She also watched the man and woman in the mirror. "Excuse me," she said to Craig. "Is that your father?" She pointed to the mirror.

Craig looked at her, then at the mirror. "Yes. The one sitting with the starry-eyed woman."

"The starry-eyed woman is my mother." She lifted her glass, then fumbled in her purse, allowing him agonizing time to ponder his response. "I'm keeping an eye on her too, protecting her from lecherous old men."

"Oh, that Dad was a lecher," Craig said.

"I didn't mean to eavesdrop, but I heard what you said about women on dating sites. They don't hold a monopoly on creative expression."

Craig stood and walked toward her. "Craig's the name, in case you and I end up being bridesmaid and best man."

"I'm Danielle." She extended her hand. "And it's not likely I'll see you at the altar. Mother's not looking for a long-term relationship."

Craig looked in the mirror. "They never are. Not until the second date. But it looks like they're getting along. She has her hand on his sleeve."

"Don't jump to conclusions. She's a touchy-feely person."

"So you have experience with dating sites?" Craig asked.

"Unfortunately, yes. And may I add a few entries to your lexicon? 'Looking for friendship' means looking for sex. 'Exercises 3 to 5 times a week' means walking from the parking lot to the bar. And 'A few extra pounds' means if you tell him to haul ass, he has to make two trips."

The bartender raised his eyebrows. "Craig, you've met your match."

"Wait a minute," Craig said. "Were you listed on E-compatible? I recognize you. You're Naughty Marietta. But I thought you were blond."

"That was then."

"And I thought you were . . ." He paused. "I thought you were petite."

"So did I. And who are you? Don't tell me you're Magic Fingers?"

"Magic Fingers?" The bartender raised a glass. "I love it."

"So what happened to you?" Craig asked. "You just dropped off the site."

"No, I didn't. It was your turn to respond. I thought you found Ms. Wonderful."

From the dining room, Mr. Barnes looked in the mirror of the bar and saw Craig sitting close to a woman. "I'd better keep an eye on my son," he said. "That's him with the starry-eyed woman clinging to him."

"Interesting," she said. "That starry-eyed woman is my daughter."

WEATHER

It wasn't Kate's idea to buy the tavern last summer. But it was the only tavern Jim could afford, if he could afford this one. She had seniority at Kmart, was thought of as management material. But Jim, her husband, he had this wild hair up his ass that someday he'd own a tavern. No thought about rookie hired help that robbed you blind, or liability insurance that cost a bundle, or a liquor license that renewed yearly at the whim of the city council. None of that.

This town at the edge of the prairie wasn't her idea either. Winter six months of the year. Snow. Naked stretches of cropland to the north that give the arctic headwinds a free ride, pounding the tavern, sculpting snow banks around the entry, blocking the parking lot. This is not where she hoped to set down her roots, to *be fruitful and multiply.*

And the patrons, as motley a crew as can be rallied. A typical assembly here tonight. Kate doesn't know their names, never bothered to learn them. She calls them Weatherman, Motor Head, and Mr. Conspiracy, which is what everyone calls them. Weatherman is front and center, what with a forecast of the storm of the century threatening. Motor Head allows as how his GMC four-wheel-drive pickup will make it through damn near anything winter can throw. Conspiracy sits alone at the end of the bar. No one listens to his current tirade against Big Pharm which has a cure for cancer but is keeping it under wraps.

And where is Jim tonight? Home, of course, watching the Timberwolves. He could have watched the game here at the tavern, but the regulars are not basketball fans, preferring the weather channel with its repeating maps of drifting cold fronts and dissecting isobars.

Wind rams the tavern's north wall and lights flicker. "Doesn't look good," Weatherman says. "Could be in for a big one. Hope you got some candles," he yells to Kate.

The phone rings. "Power is out here at the house," Jim says. "Right when the Wolves were ready to rally. Likely to lose telephone lines too. Anything going on there?"

"What am I to do if the power fails?" She hears a buzz. "Hello? Hello?"

"Doesn't sound good," says Weatherman.

Motor Head grins like he's found the lost chord. "You got a generator?"

"How the hell would I know?" Kate turns and leans on the cash register.

A blast of north wind thrusts the door open exposing a waist-high drift on the stoop. Weatherman rotates off his stool and scrambles to close it. "Damn. This is serious. I should've figured we'd be in for trouble with that east wind today. It's a bad omen."

"Not to worry," says Motor Head. "I'll get everybody home."

Weatherman downs his beer. "No one in his right mind would go out in this stuff."

Kate monitors the television. A blizzard warning for this part of the state. *High winds. Drifting snow. Falling temperatures. Travel not advised.* She rummages through the emergency drawer for a flashlight and spots a billy club which she removes.

"Pour us another round, Kate," says Weatherman. "One for you and one for the Grand Conspirator too."

Kate pours for the men and a blackberry brandy for herself. "Has this happened before? A power failure in a blizzard?"

"Hell, yes," says Weatherman. "It happened all the time when Sully owned the bar. Mostly 'cause he didn't pay his electric bill. He kept a box of candles in the drawer with the telephone books. I expect they're still there."

Kate finds a box of votive candles and places them around the bar and one beside the cash register.

"You won't need that cash register if the power goes out," Motor Head says.

"Good old Sully," Weatherman continues. "Used to plunk the Old Crow down right here when the lights went out, and he'd take a stool right there. We'd sit out the storm, and nobody left 'til it quit or the break of dawn, whichever came first."

"That's why Sully is history," Kate says.

"That's why Sully is legend," says Weatherman.

Another blast of wind, and the sign that hangs over the stoop scrapes and scratches. "Must've snapped the guy wires," Motor Head says. "Look at that north wall. It's heavin' in those gusts. Wonder how long the old studs will take it."

"Don't worry about us old studs," Weatherman says. "Age and cunning will trump youth and vigor any day. But I think we've got a date with destiny tonight. And there's the four of us. We've got a quorum. How 'bout you, Mr. Conspirator? Wanna comment on global warming?"

"Or how about the real story that Detroit and the oil companies are covering up? That there's an engine out there good for a hundred miles a gallon," Motor Head adds.

Another gust of wind, and the door heaves open again. Kate ducks below the counter and hears someone rush to close the door. The overhead lights flicker; the neons go dark. Now it's black. Kate flicks her cigarette lighter and lights candles. *Damn that Jim. Him and his big ideas. And where is he? Sitting in front of the wood stove, warm and toasty, sippin' a Baileys.*

"Well, the good news is that we're not going to die of thirst," Weatherman says.

"Do you think we're safe in here?" Kate asks.

"When your time's up, your time's up." Motor Head raises his glass in a toast. "To mortality. Long may it wave."

"Put it this way," Weatherman says. "You'll last a helluva lot longer in here than you would out there."

Kate carries a candle and walks from behind the bar to the window. Total darkness. A clatter of snow and sleet scratches the glass; a draft of frigid air chills her face. The candle flickers and dies. The aroma of hot wax transports her. Birthday cakes. Christmas dinner. Benediction at St. Mary's.

"Better get away from the window," Weatherman calls.

Kate is startled, paralyzed, mute. He walks to her and leads her to a stool in front of the bar. She stares at him, stares at the other two. Weatherman rounds the corner of the bar and pours her a glass of blackberry brandy. "Drink this. It'll relax you."

She gulps and chokes and senses a familiar warmth, a pleasant sting.

"Do it again," he says, and refills her glass. "Relax. We'll get through this."

Kate plants her elbows on the bar and concentrates on a faint whistle, the wind finding a chink in the building's exterior. "I'm a fish out of water," she says to no one.

Motor Head rushes out the door, then rushes back with a tool box. The men coordinate their efforts, like they know the drill. They push the pool table and jukebox against the wall. They tip tables on their sides and prop one against the door. They open cardboard cartons, flatten them, and tack them over windows. Kate pours another blackberry brandy and stares at the bar. Beside a candle, a huge Culligan bottle sits stuffed with donated coins and bills for the Mattson boy's surgery.

Her abbreviated Kmart career crops up. Her colleagues—the community college dropouts, the desperate housewives who needed to break away from the old man and the kids. Or to get an employee discount at Christmas. People she spoke to less after a couple years than she speaks to these customers. And trusted less than that.

"I don't know your names," she cries.

"I'm Will," Weatherman answers. "That's Manny." He points his hammer handle toward Motor Head. "And that's Al." He points to Mr. Conspiracy.

"Aren't you married?" Her voice cracks. "Aren't you worried about your wives?" She pushes her glass forward and slouches to the bar. Her shoulders shudder; her fingers tighten around her arms. "Aren't they worried about you?"

Morning. Kate awakens to a pounding on the door, a table moving, footsteps across the floor. She lays on seat cushions, covered with her coat. Her pillow is a couple rolls of paper toweling. Her mouth is dry, her tongue swollen and tasting of putrid berries. She raises her head to see Jim in the door, his snowmobile suit silhouetted against a lemon morning sun. The tavern is dark and disheveled, furniture stacked against walls, papered windows.

"Kate, where are you?" Jim pulls off his helmet.

"We made a bed for her at the end of the bar," Will says. "She damn near lost it in the storm. Was restless as a cat all night. We kept an eye on her."

Kate sits up, checks the buttons on her blouse, checks that they're buttoned in the right buttonholes.

Will watches her recover, watches her puzzlement over what may have happened. He deflects a chuckle to Manny. "I hope we didn't disappoint her."

"I know what you're thinking." Jim walks to her, his palms raised to fend off her contempt. "We'll sell this place. Move back to town."

Kate looks at her husband, looks at Will, looks at Al snoring and asleep, looks at Manny lying on the floor under the pool table cover, resting on one elbow, grinning.

Kate hadn't believed in personal saviors, never had been out of control and dependent, never appreciated fundamental survival skills. She feels sudden kinship, maybe friendship with these scrubs.

Jim reaches for her, offers his hands to help her rise. "Don't be angry with me, I know what you're thinking."

No, you don't know what I'm thinking. You don't have the slightest idea.

Story

THEME AND VARIATIONS

From the window beside her bed, Lorraine looked out to see a clump of dry leaves, an oval shape the size of a man's scruffy head, staring from the Xs and Ys of naked winter branches. Below, wind-cleared snow on the dome of the charcoal grill left the north edge exposed.

Male pattern baldness, thought Lorraine. *Louie, when will you leave me alone?*

She rose, eager to dispel the image, to shrug off the feelings. In the kitchen, she snapped on the radio and measured coffee grounds. A pot for one. Reassurance in solitude.

Lorraine surveyed the kitchen, the uncluttered countertops, the empty sink, the bare burners on the stove. Her kitchen now, not Louie's. A week ago, pasta canisters lined the walls. A large ceramic apple cookie jar held biscotti. A popcorn bowl sat in the sink, the unpopped kernels sticking to empty Budweiser cans.

I don't miss that, she mused. But the blandness of birch cupboards, linen walls, and ivory countertops struck her as a metaphor for life—monochromatic and dull.

Louie, she thought. *When will you leave me alone?*

Luigi ("call me Louie") flooded her with compliments when they met. He was older, mid-thirties; Lorraine admitted to twenty-four. They were different, but she was comfortable in his company. His rough edges contrasted with her well-honed manners. His tastes, his talk were unaffected. What first she considered boorish, she later found authentic and refreshing. As did her friends.

His down-home expressions, his Mario Lanza impersonation embarrassed her, then charmed her. "Your vocabulary is richer than pecan pie," she mocked. "Your Sicilian vernacular tickles me."

Louie turned aside and faked embarrassment. "Hell, I don't talk no different from nobody else. We may be horses of a different color,

but we're all eggs in the same basket."

Lorraine laughed. "You sound like my granddad."

Now Louie was gone, like the other ones. Gone, and with him, the aroma of fresh basil, the boxes of potato chips, the apple cookie jar. She was alone, like the Lorraine she knew best.

The phone rang. "What's wrong?" her mother asked when Lorraine answered. "I can tell by your voice that's something's wrong."

"Louie left."

Silence. Then, "How long did *he* last? Since last winter? You and *TIME* magazine should get together on your Man of the Year."

"I wasn't asking for sympathy, Mother."

"That's good, because I don't have any. Not for you after two marriages and more affairs than I can count. You couldn't even get along with your father."

Lorraine thought about Dad. No word from him since he walked away. Maybe dead, maybe alive. She remembered the last day she saw him, standing in the kitchen of the duplex in St. Cloud. He was stirring spaghetti sauce, wearing a red silk Hawaiian shirt and Elvis Presley sideburns. She was a high school senior and had argued with him over a weekend curfew. Her mother leaned over the sink washing dishes, keeping her distance.

"Well, Mother," her dad had said. "Are you going to support me on this one?" He tilted his head at a quizzical angle.

Her mother dried her hands on an apron. "I think you two can work it out."

"I don't think we can," he said. "I'm tired of being the lonely little onion in this petunia patch." Next morning, he was gone.

"He'll be back," her mother said. "He's done this before."

He didn't return. Lorraine replayed the conversation, regretted her insolence, felt distance between her and her mother. Over coffee one morning, her mother said, "If you hadn't been such a bitch . . ."

Lorraine stewed over her mother's stinging comment and her dad's departure, staying away from men until she met Harold at a Christmas party. The fact that he was thirty-two and paid her attention was flattering. He wanted children, he said. Lots of children. And she was the right age to fulfill his ambition.

After their first night together, she was convinced she was pregnant. The symptoms her friends discussed—dizziness, morning

112

sickness, food craving—all of these presented themselves at confusing moments, in bewildering deportment. She confided in Harold, not her mother.

"We have to get married," Lorraine said. "As soon as I graduate." She had rehearsed this speech for days. "Mother will want a church wedding. The baby should be born around Christmas. If it's a boy, we'll call him Harold, Jr." All of which played into Harold's plan.

Later, the doctor told Lorraine that stress had caused her to miss her period—her father's leaving, her mother's hostility, her graduation, Harold's arrival. The doctor offered his diagnosis before the wedding.

Lorraine mulled it. Her friends would snicker if she backed out. Her mother would roll her eyes. Harold would be despondent; he had bought a Jenny Lind crib at the used furniture store. Besides, she would likely be pregnant next month. They married.

But she wasn't pregnant. When Harold heard the gynecologist say Lorraine was infertile, and when she confessed the pregnancy ploy, he had the marriage annulled. Lorraine found a job as a file clerk and moved into a *No Men Allowed* boarding house.

She met Darrin weeks later at a friend's wedding. Bridesmaid Lorraine loved the bridal showers, the lunches, the ceremony, the gaudy extravagance. Her speech defined hyperbole. A French braid was the *most* elegant, a bouquet the *most* glorious, an organ prelude the *most* breathtaking. In this giddy whirlwind, Lorraine considered Darrin to be the *most* handsome of the groomsmen, albeit an inch shorter than her.

Lorraine danced with Darrin at the reception and found him comfortably uncomfortable. "Do you know this step?" she asked when the DJ played a waltz. When he didn't, she led. She locked her arms around him, stood tall, moved him around the floor like a doll.

"I'm warm," she said, lowering her dress off the rounds of her shoulders when the song ended. "Let's get some air."

Within months, they married, at Lorraine's suggestion. "He's so malleable," she told her friends. "One hundred sixty pounds of Silly Putty. You want plain vanilla, he's plain vanilla. You want tutti-frutti, he's tutti-frutti. Nothing beyond tutti-frutti though. Nothing imaginative, nothing exotic."

"Have you taught him to sit on the toilet instead of peeing on the floor?" someone asked.

"I should. I will."

Lorraine returned from work to find a note on the kitchen table. "I'm sorry. So sorry. I can't seem to satisfy you," it read. "I tried to be charitable with you, to be flexible. But you treat me like a dog. Maybe that's what you should have—a dog. Maybe I'll buy one for you. I'll start the proceedings. I'm sorry."

Lorraine met Luigi at an Italian cooking class, where they were assigned the salad course. Louie tore the lettuce with the fingers of a masseur, diced the tomatoes with staccato precision, sliced the onion paper thin, and tossed the ingredients with theatric abandon. Lorraine sipped Chianti and watched his fingers gently crumble the feta cheese and fondle the Kalamata olives.

"You like to cook, don't you?" she asked at dinner.

"I allow myself one bad habit. Food."

And now Louie was gone. The cast iron cookware, the German cutlery, the kitchen planter of fresh herbs. The aroma of sauces when she walked in the door, the aria from *La Boheme*, the bear hug welcome. Gone. All gone.

Her mother joined her for coffee Saturday morning. "It's good to have the condo to myself," Lorraine said. "No tripping over his stuff. No explaining if I want to go to bed at eight. Get up at three."

Her mother sipped coffee.

"I've had it with men," Lorraine continued. "Toilet seats left up. Monday night football. Whiskers in the bathroom sink."

Her mother yawned.

"I can live without them." Lorraine cradled her coffee cup and stared out the window. The phone rang. "You're kidding, Tony," she said when she answered. "A round trip to Las Vegas? For two? You lucky guy. Sure, I'll go." She listened. "I've never stayed at the MGM Grand."

Her mother tapped her cup on the table and glared.

"Let me arrange a few things," Lorraine said to the phone. "I'll call you tonight."

CHARADES

The scene opens with a woman sitting on a boulder beside a large lake in morning fog. She cradles her knees. Wind blows her hair and waves her scarf. She clutches a cup of coffee. Cresting waves spray the air. A man stands behind her, hands in pockets, staring at the water, bracing into the breeze.

She: My friends at the office are so jealous. They said it sounds like a second honeymoon. Just the two of us. No kids. No telephone. No schedule. If they only knew. Right, Darling?"

He: If they only knew what?

She: Don't be coy. We're adults. We can handle it.

She sets the mug on the boulder rubs her hands to warm them. In a low voice, says,

She: I forgot my rings.

In a loud voice,

She: I'm glad we brought these mugs.

She lifts her mug.

She: Didn't we steal them from a coffee shop in Santé Fe?"

He: We didn't steal them. We borrowed them.

She: I stole mine. Let's not argue. Let's talk.

He: I don't want to talk this morning. I'll drive you into town for breakfast. Then perhaps I'll rent a sailboat for the afternoon. Would you like that?

She: It's too cold to sail. Unless you want to take me far out on the lake and drown me.

He: Don't be ridiculous.

She: It would solve your problem.

He: Stop it. I'm walking back to the lodge.

She: Don't leave. We have to talk about it sometime.

She waves to a couple walking hand in hand along the shore, cups her hands

THAT REMINDS ME

and yells,
She: Good Morning.

     She turns to the lake.

She: I love the taste of the air, don't you, Darling? Fresh. Natural. Healthy. Not salty like the coast of Maine. I want to inhale and exhale until I've flushed out all the evil and hurt inside. Don't you feel that?
He: It's good air.
She: And these rocks. These huge boulders. Black and wet. Imagine the power that moved them. They look like whales. Beached whales.
He: I'm not wearing my watch. What time is it?
She: Please. Sit by me. Tell me how you feel. Or what you fear.
He: I fear nothing. It's clumsy. And the timing is terrible.
She: The timing is always terrible.
He: It's especially terrible now. I'm close to landing the new position. It wouldn't look good if we proceeded.
She: Would it look better six months from now? A year? That's selfish of you.
He: No, not selfish at all. My salary increase would benefit you too.

     He stands behind her and runs his fingers through her windblown hair.

He: And we have to think of the kids. Jane leaves for college next year. Jodie starts high school in the fall. We owe them a stable home life.
She: Delay because of the job? Delay because of the kids? I don't remember that in my wedding vows.

     She reaches for a small rock at her feet and tosses it in the lake.

She: Take that back. For better or for worse. I remember that.
He: Don't be cruel. Don't punish me.

     She stands and faces the lake, hands on her hips. A wave crests and crashes at her feet.

She: Is this the image of marriage we want to convey to the girls?
He: I didn't hear you. What did you say?
She: Nothing.

     She scans the horizon. The morning fog lifts to reveal a lighthouse further up the shoreline.

SEVEN

A one-scene play set in a coffee shop

She: I can't believe you're doing this. Won't this be number seven?

He: Dolly, Margaret Mary, Krystal, Alexis, Jo, Trish. I guess you're right.

She: Has it occurred to you that you weren't meant to be married?

He: No. *Au contraire . . .*

She: You know what you are? You're a serial monogamist. I leave town for a few years thinking I can trust you, and what happens? You change spouses faster than you change socks.

He: Wait a minute. You make it sound like I'm making my seventh mistake. I'd say I'm embarking on my seventh adventure. I'm fulfilling myself with seven life-changing experiences.

She: It's not all about you. You're leaving a trail of broken hearts, betrayed innocents, used women.

He: Not true. My first two marriages ended in annulments. Remember Dolly from our senior year at Roosevelt High? Dolly was my first love. My first infatuation, at least. We were kids, underage when we got married. It was a kind of extra credit project for Modern Problems. Dolly's parents had the marriage annulled when they found out.

She: I envied her at the time, but I've tried to forget that.

He: Then Margaret Mary. Her parents had the marriage annulled when they discovered I wasn't Catholic. I told them I was agnostic. They asked if that was a branch of The Church. I told them it was like Russian Orthodox. That was good enough for them as long as I agreed to raise our kids Catholic. Of course I would. Sure. Catholic. Like Lent. And altar boys. Meatless Fridays. Bingo in the church basement. I loved Margaret Mary too. More of a platonic love. What else could it be with their prescribed rhythm method?

She: I hear you, but that doesn't let you off the hook.

He: I stayed single for months after that. My next marriage ended in divorce. Krystal was a manager at Blue Cross. She felt she was being passed over for promotion because she was single. Didn't match the company's image of family values. I met her on a dating site for professionals. We had a great time while it lasted. I sported a brand new wardrobe. Was squired around in a company car. Sat in box seats at Viking games. When she was promoted to VP, she bought me out.

She: And of course you loved her too.

He: Yes, yes, yes. We're still pals. But then I met Alexis on Friend Finder. Alexis was Russian and wanted citizenship. I knew going in that she hadn't planned on a lifetime commitment, but I hoped to change her mind and convert her to democracy. She was exotic. And mysterious. And chaste. We rented a two-bedroom apartment. She had her room and I had mine. We shared a bath, but when she used it, she locked the door. It pains me to confess this, but we never consummated our marriage.

She: You of all people. And now, you're in damage control.

He: She tired of my amorous advances. It was always her time of month. Then she announced she had an infectious disease and taped a quarantine sign on her door. Right next to the portraits of Khrushchev and Trotsky.

She: And all the while, you thought you'd convert her.

He: I persevered. She invited her communist friends to the apartment and they spoke Russian all night. They ignored me. All I did was pour their vodka. The day she was granted citizenship, she hosted a party and said I wasn't invited. She changed locks on the door. Wouldn't answer my phone calls. But I couldn't forget her. I sent her roses. I loved that woman. I followed her to work until she had me arrested for stalking.

She: I'm starting to see a pattern. My old friend is a plaything of the gods.

He: Thank heavens I met Jo soon after.

She: Jo. Wasn't she the biker gal?

He: Yes, she was. No limits for that woman. No inhibitions. No sacred cows. I loved it. We fenced the back yard and cavorted around naked guzzling Jack Daniels out of a bottle and blaring Bruce Springsteen. I loved her freedom. I loved her passion. I loved everything but her hair.

She: Hair? I remember she had short hair. A mannish cut.

He: Right. I'm talking facial hair. I should have listened to my dad. He said beware of the woman who can grow a better beard than you.

She: That's terrible.

He: She rode with a group called Bikers for Christ. To keep their image, they didn't allow singles to cohabit on their trips.

She: So you got married?

He: Right. For a wedding present, she bought me the complete black leather outfit. I couldn't afford my own bike and she wouldn't let me drive hers, so I rode on the back seat while she drove. Of course, both of us dressed the same, and she being bigger than me, no one gave it a thought. Strangers looked twice though when we pulled into a rest stop, and she headed for the ladies' room. I . . . I . . .

She: You're choking up

He: I miss Jo. Came time for the Sturgis Rally, and I couldn't get time off from work. So she rode with the Christ bikers. She collided with a cattle truck on some South Dakota highway. Want to wear her leathers?

She: Tell me we're getting close to the end of your story.

He: Yes, we are. Finally, there was Trish. I guess I hadn't been forthright with Trish before we married. When she found she was number six, she went into deep depression. We spent months with a psychiatrist. Spent a fortune on anti-depressants. We practically lived with the marriage counselor. In desperation, I asked if she would like me to disappear, maybe jump out a first-story window. She said that sounded like a great idea. So what did she do?

She: Jumped out a first-story window.

He: She jumped out a window, but not the first story.

She: Enough. Enough. Why are you telling me this?

He: Well . . . I met Jane and we hit it off. She's my primary care physician's nurse, and when she was updating the file for my annual physical, she kind of strayed from the printed questions. Like, are you married? No. Are you single, widowed, or divorced? Yes. Yes. Yes. Are you depressed? No. Are you lonely? Well, yes, I am lonely, sometimes. She said she facilitates a support group for people like me. Would I like to attend? I said sure, let's talk about it over dinner. You have to understand Jane is plain. No makeup. Drives a tan Chevy Malibu. Still lives with her mom and dad. Watches reruns of *Leave it to Beaver*.

She: Wait a minute. You hustled your doctor's nurse?

He: No. It was a professional conversation. She agreed to dinner, and guess what she ordered? Mac and cheese. She constantly asked about my health. Was I eating a proper diet? Was I sleeping eight hours a night? Did I smoke? What was my alcohol consumption? How did I manage stress? I could see she was a caregiver. A tender loving caregiver.

She: Let me guess. You fell in love with her and now you want to marry her.

He: Kind of. But this time it isn't love. That's where I made my mistakes. I always married for love. This time I'm being practical. This time I'm planning ahead. Someday, I won't be able to care for myself. She's much younger than me. I'll have a built-in private nurse in my golden years.

She: This is incredible. My stomach is in knots. We've been friends forever. Why are you telling me this?

He: I was getting around to that. We're planning a honeymoon, but, no surprise, Jane is afraid to fly. And she hates to be away from work more than a few days. So we're wondering if we could borrow your cabin on the North Shore for a long weekend.

She: Look. I can't let you go through with this. You're a great guy. You're witty. You're sensitive. You're presentable. You're my lifetime friend. You were there for me during my divorce. God, how many times did I call you? I care about you. I want you to be fulfilled. You can't marry someone just to empty your bedpans. I'd marry you myself if that would make you happy.

He: You would? Great. I was hoping you'd say that.

WOODWORK

Clay didn't know when his love life began to unravel. Come to think of it, he didn't know when it began. All he knew is that she took the lead, and now it was over. Like a summer storm that roiled in with gusts of energy, he bent to accommodate the onslaught, sudden darkness blinding everything around him, howls of thunder, spasms of lightning. And then, quiet. Life resumed. What was all the drama?

Years ago Desiree's mother Verne, a Brownsville gal with big intentions and ambition but limited talent and smarts, had moved to the Big Apple to be a star. "Gonna show you folks," she said. "Gonna show you where big ideas can take you."

Where was that? Back to Brownsville. The only role she landed was motherhood, the price she paid for an audition as a chorus girl. Now she lived her star-struck life styling the local blue-haired ladies at her Salon Chic, reading dog-eared copies of *People* and *Cosmopolitan*.

Desiree had two strikes against her, trying to lead her life and her mother's. She auditioned for lead in the junior high class play and lost. Took voice lessons and never soloed in Glee Club. Took gymnastics and couldn't land a spot as cheerleader for the hapless Brownsville Bears.

She had hair, not always a predictable style or color, and eye shadow and cashmere sweaters. If you were the new kid in town, you'd think she was Miss Popularity. Wrong. She knew how to win whistles from the guys, but gals shunned her. "Jealous," her mother said.

Clay's turn to sample her charms came on graduation day. Clay, the virgin farm kid, flattered when she invited him to her party, dumbfounded when she slow-danced with him in her garage ball room, shocked when she suggested some hanky-panky if he'd stick around later that night. Bewildered after a whirlwind courtship, then moving in together and making wedding plans.

"Don't do this," Verne said. "Don't limit your options."

Who knows what drummer's beat Desiree was marching to? Who knows if she missed her mother's doting, her inspiration, her praise? Who knows if she wanted more than babies and dirty laundry and a rusted Ford Falcon?

Clay didn't know. They forfeited the one-month rent deposit and moved home, Clay to his, Desiree to hers. "Chalk it up," his buddies said. "You're just one more notch in her headboard."

WATCH

All this happened in the early eighties when we knew every neighbor in town. Outsiders were rare and warranted a skeptical and watchful eye when they entered the Erickson Grocery or Main Street Cafe.

Our house was a small bungalow at the edge of town, the Skelly gas station to the right, a sweet corn field to the left. Across the street, an abandoned feed mill sagged and rotted and housed a hundred pigeons.

I would be a high school senior in the fall. Mom was the only divorced woman in town and, back then, the object of speculation among both men and women. She worked at Prairie Bar & Grill, a waitress by day and barmaid on weekend nights. It may have been her independent spirit that caused speculation, or it may have been her snug T-shirts. Whatever the reason, tip money at the Bar & Grill exceeded her wages. I was unmindful of her wardrobe and body until the Skelly gas attendant said, "Your mom's got great knockers."

Mom wanted to leave Jones Prairie and had saved a few bucks each paycheck to buy a house in a bigger town, maybe the city. She wanted a higher paying job, and she wanted me to attend college when I graduated. She wasn't naïve about finances, nor was she willing to place us on public assistance although we might have qualified. She had her eye on St. Cloud where factories were hiring, and the community college would be a walk from home. She bought the *St. Cloud Herald* at Johnson's Drug and checked the want ads for real estate.

"We're never going to afford any of this at the rate I'm saving," she said. "We're gonna have a garage sale. Get rid of some of this junk we've accumulated. You!" She pointed at me. "Be thinking about your old bike, the clothes you've outgrown. Books, ice skates, baseball bats, anything."

From the tone of her voice, I knew she had thought this out, that the sale would happen soon. "I've decided to sell Great Grandfather's Civil War pocket watch." she said. "We'll advertise it as an antique. Get some of that big city money." She hummed when she felt conviction, and she hummed now.

The watch had caused contention in the family since Mom's Grandma willed it to her. We knew the watch was worth about $2,000 after Mom had it appraised. Her mistake was sharing that information with the family. "That should be about $500 apiece," I remember my Aunt Ruth saying. She stopped visiting us after that, maybe remembering us with a Christmas card, maybe not.

"You're selling the watch?" I said. "It's an heirloom. Your sister will hate you."

"She'll never know," Mom said.

I knew a lot about the watch, knew a lot about my great, great grandfather Silas Slayton, a sergeant in the Civil War. I wrote a research paper about him for English, got an A. He served with the 3rd Minnesota Regiment, Company F, in Nashville, Tennessee. A dour-looking gentleman in the Company's sepia photograph, with a handlebar mustache and a mean glint in his eye. Mom told stories she heard about him, about his trigger temper and cruelty toward his team of horses. "I'm giving you this watch with a disclaimer," Grandmother had told Mom. "My father was an evil man, and I wouldn't be surprised if the watch is cursed."

Maybe it was. Mom split with Dad the summer she inherited it. Then she totaled the car when she hit a deer in the fall. In winter, she slipped on ice and broke her shoulder and lost her job. I heard Aunt Ruth say when visiting Mom in the hospital, "Serves her right."

Mom scheduled the garage sale for the Fourth of July weekend when city folk would be driving north through town to resorts and cabins. We cleaned the garage, loaded tables and benches with folded sweaters, dish towels, and blankets, and hung jeans and pantsuits and the ugly green and orange afghan on a wire clothes line. Mom surprised me by hanging a formal gown, worn as a bridesmaid years ago, she said. I pictured her wearing it, burgundy satin, off-the-shoulder neck line. I could hear the swishing sound of the skirt as she paraded up the church aisle.

We pounded *Garage Sale—Antiques* signs at the intersections of Main Street on Thursday night and opened for business Friday morning. I sat at the garage door behind a card table with a cupcake

124

pan for coin change and a cigar box for bills. Mom plugged in Mr. Coffee and stacked paper cups and a creamer and sugar bowl on the tool bench. Neighbors, lured by the aroma of coffee, were first to drop by, fingering merchandise and offering small talk. "I remember when you wore this blouse." "You're getting rid of these dishes?"

Mom had set up a display near my checkout table with a sign ANTIQUES. She arranged jewelry on a black velvet cushion. She aligned Indian Head pennies under a sheet of glass. She placed a porcelain doll music box on a pedestal and lifted the "on" switch when a potential customer walked by. In a small wooden chest, the Civil War watch resided, polished to a soft silver gleam and open to expose the Roman numeral dial. A sign *Genuine P. S. Bartlett Civil War Pocket Watch, 1857* stood before it.

Cars arrived and customers looked and talked, but weren't buying. Mom hummed and smiled reassurance at me as she refolded aprons and pillow cases and chatted with neighbors. "You can always use an extra frying pan," she'd say to a woman at the housewares table. Or, "That color looks good on you," to a woman pressing a dress to her body in front of the mirror.

A black Buick Roadmaster pulled into the driveway and parked on the lawn, away from other cars. People stopped talking and stared— we hadn't seen this car before. A man stepped from the driver's side, a woman from the passenger side. The man was built like Tweedle Dum with ink black hair. He stood by the car, leaning against the hood, and crossed his thin, pale arms.

The woman was tall and wore a black pantsuit. Her wrists were tanned to brown and jangled with silver bracelets. She strutted to the garage and, as she passed, her musky perfume startled me. It followed her like fog. She was careful to avoid contact with the tables, reaching at a cup and saucer but not touching it. "Where are the antiques?" she called to Mom.

"They're over here." I heard cash register bells ringing in Mom's voice above her humming.

The woman walked to the table and pointed to the watch. "How do you know it's genuine?"

"It was Great Grandfather's. We had it appraised." She handed the watch to the lady. "Do you see the serial number? 30515. It's a key wind, and this is the key."

The woman inspected the watch.

"Do you see the inscription on the cover?" Mom asked. "Sgt. Silas Slayton, 3rd Minnesota Regiment."

The woman seemed not to hear.

"It appraised for $2,000, but we're willing to let it go for $1,500."

The woman pulled glasses from her pocket and held the watch close to her face. She looked at Mom with distrust. "Let me show this to my husband." She put the watch in the wooden chest and walked, not waiting for Mom's approval.

"Keep an eye on her," Mom said. She wasn't humming. "We don't want to lose our ticket to Happy Land."

I watched the lady. The man was sitting in the Buick now, a phone pressed to his ear. I had heard about the new portable bag phones, knew they were expensive, knew it would be years before they found their way to Jones Prairie.

The woman returned after a few minutes. "Can we have your phone number?" she asked. "My husband wants to call an antique dealer friend and get an opinion of the watch's value. We'll call you if we're interested."

Mom gave her our number, and the woman walked to the car. She returned and asked to see the watch again. "My husband wants to describe it to our antique dealer friend," she said, and placed the watch in its chest and walked.

The telephone rang, and Mom rushed toward the house. "Keep an eye on Mrs. High Maintenance," she said. "I'll be right back."

I heard her conversation on the telephone. "Yes, take a right off Main Street at Fourth Avenue. The last house on the street, next to the Skelly station." And after a pause, "We'll be open until five or six, whenever the customers stop coming." Another pause, and "No, no tools, I'm afraid. Sporting goods, women's and boys' clothes, household things."

The woman returned the watch chest and placed it on the table. "My husband said it's not worth $1,500." She strode to the car, slid in, and the car pulled away.

Mom walked back to the garage. "Some man wanted a lot of information about our garage sale." She looked at the chest sitting on the antiques table. "Looks like she didn't want the watch."

"She said her husband didn't think it was worth $1,500."

Mom walked to the table, not humming. She opened the chest. Empty. She turned to the street, looking for the black Buick. "Damn," she yelled. "Damn, damn, damn."

Then she was quiet. She poured a cup of coffee and sat next to me.

"What do we do now?" I asked, "Call the cops?"

"No." In a while, she was humming again. "No. I'm glad to be rid of the damn thing. I'm not superstitious, but my luck took a turn for the worse the day Grandma gave it to me."

I saw her smile, her chin-high confidence, her chest-out independence. She went back to refolding sweaters in neat rows.

I looked at the intense July sky, hoping for a shaft of sunlight to appear through the box elders, a bluebird to sing, the crabapple tree to burst into mysterious bloom. Instead pigeons swooped in wide formation around the abandoned feed mill and crows cawed in the sweet corn field. Mom hummed her way into the house to refill Mr. Coffee.

LEGEND OF THE SKULL

Prehistoric Bison Remains Found in U.S. 71 Extension
Menahga Messenger *headline, July 1950*

*A portion of a human skull was found by persons canoeing on the Crow Wing River near
Cottingham Park. They reported their discovery to the Sheriff's Department, and deputies
recovered the remains. Test results determined that the skull was between 600 and 700 years old.*
Sebeka-Menahga Review Messenger, *September 2002*

Before the sun opened, the sky was a rubble of clouds the color of summer flowers and autumn maples. A crow announced the birth of day. Young coyotes yelped from faraway woods. Another pack answered. Then it was quiet, still.

Dew-dampened grass quieted a crouching band of hunters. They advanced, one by one, in an arc, each carrying two sapling poles. On the end of the poles, a thong held brilliant feathers and scraps of fur. The hunting party was large—all the men of the village.

Within the arc of hunters, a bull buffalo stood sleeping, his shaggy head drooping to the ground, his horns catching the glint of early morning sun. Cows and calves lay sleeping. The hunting party arced from a creek bed to encircle the sleeping herd. When the arc was complete, the lead hunter Big Bear sprang from the grass. All the hunters stood, waving their poles, running toward the herd, whooping, shrieking, chanting. The buffalo stumbled and scrambled away from the encircling hunters into the creek bed. The mud slowed their advance. The bull, biggest and heaviest, propelled by his speed lunged forward and churned the mud in an attempt to rise. A cow followed. Her calf, lighter and buoyed by clumps of cattails, advanced toward the stream, tripped, and lay tangled and trembling.

The hunters charged the struggling prey, dropped their poles, and brandished flint lances and knives. Big Bear hopped, hummock to hummock, to the bull, straddled him, and drove a knife into his neck.

The bull bolted and bucked, twisting his massive head in a

frenzied arc. He forced a front leg forward, kicked with the rear. Big Bear felt the bull's struggle for survival, felt the bull's hot muscled body through his leggings, smelled his musky sweat. He grabbed a massive horn in one hand and forced the knife deeper, deeper. His hand was red with heady, intoxicating blood. The bull bucked with his last burst of strength, then lowered his head and trembled his final quakes.

Big Bear twisted the bull's head and met his dying gaze. He inhaled the final snorts of hot breath, then lay silent, still astraddle the bull. He pulled the bloodied knife from the bull's neck, raised his bloodied arms and hands, and released the bull's spirit into the morning sky.

Calves scrambled toward the water and belly-crawled through reeds. Younger hunters followed, hopping from earth clod to clod. Young Bear Paw reached a calf, jumped on his back, and brought him to his belly in mud. Bear Paw arced his knife as his father had instructed and felt the calf surrender. He lifted the calf's head out of muck as it struggled and gasped, then crawled forward until his head was over the dying animal's nostrils to breathe its dying breath.

Butchering was quiet and efficient. Hunters dragged the buffaloes from mud to dry ground, skinned and gutted them, and divided the carcasses into transportable-sized chunks. Other men laced the sapling poles together into travois. The hides and flesh were divided among the hunters, and the horns and a shock of hair were cut from the skulls. By the time the sun was high, the hunters formed a procession home, along the creek bed to where it joined the Cat River and along the river to where the Cat joined the larger river known as Raven's Wing.

Bear Paw and his father assembled a harness of dried buffalo skins, knotted it to the travois, and slipped the straps over their shoulders. One moon and another sun would appear before they returned to the village. They pulled as equals, in lock step, over the path of flattened reeds and grass toward the woods where the sun rose. The procession of hunters was quiet. Their steps, quick and strong; their eyes rotated from the path ahead to the perilous woods. They plodded along the creek bed, the sun at their backs until they arrived at a site where they would camp for the night.

The hunting party set up camp in a circle, carcasses in the center. Renegade tribes of stragglers who had been ousted from their villages prowled the area and wreaked revenge by ambushing a lone hunter and robbing him of his game, or kidnapping a young berry picker who strayed beyond her mother's view.

When the hunters had built a fire near the heap of carcasses, they impaled strips of buffalo meat on sharpened sticks and roasted them in the flames. While they ate, they talked in low monotones about the leap onto the mired buffalo's back, the deftness of the swing of the knife, the labored final breath as the spirit escaped the body.

After they ate, the men huddled by the fire in the clear cold night. They filled their pipes with tobacco and smoked. Bear Paw sat behind his father, behind the ring of senior hunters. Big Bear motioned him into the circle and handed him the pipe. Trails of sparks spiraled up to the sky and returned to earth in the form of snowflakes.

In the morning, the ground was white. When Bear Paw peered from under his sleeping robe, other young men fed the fire. The party ate scraps from last night's meal and broke camp for the final day's trek to the village. The hunting party became a winding ribbon of men and travois, skirting the Cat River banks. Snow fell and covered the sun. Wind blew from the direction of the setting sun and propelled them toward the village.

When the sun was at its highest point, they stopped. Bear Paw retrieved a handful of dried cranberries from a bag tied to his leggings. He scooped drinking water from the river in a trough of birch bark. The wind blew colder, and ice formed along the shore. From upstream, scattered floes of ice scraped against the shore like flint chipping against flint.

When the sun lowered behind them, they trudged through banks of fresh snow. At intervals, the leaders of the procession would step to the side and pass the chore of breaking fresh snow to the second travois. The party would be at the mouth of the Cat River before the sun disappeared behind the pines. The wind roared and snow blew in circles. The village was a short trek ahead, where the river turned and flowed toward the Bright Star, then rounded a bend and flowed toward the Big River.

Big Bear and Bear Paw finished their rotation at the head of the procession and rested beneath an uprooted pine. The roots lifted the earth and created a shelter for small animals. Fresh rabbit tracks dotted the snow. Bear Paw thought of catching a rabbit and presenting the soft hide to his betrothed as a wedding gift. He told his plan to his father who assented. The profusion of rabbit tracks promised a quick and easy catch. Bear Paw fashioned a snare from strings of raw hide, and placed it where the tracks disappeared in the roots. He climbed atop the root clump and waited.

The hunting party continued the final leg of the trek without them, toward the smell of smoke from the huts and the riverside clearing. Mothers and children would welcome the hunting party. Tonight the aroma of fresh buffalo roasting in the huts would permeate the village. Heroic legends would be created and told for generations— the slaughter of the bull, the young buck's first kill. Women would unwrap the bulky hides and marvel at the size and warmth they would provide.

Bear Paw and his father waited at the uplifted root. The wind blew and daylight escaped the sky. Big Bear smoked his pipe and felt his son's eagerness to present a gift to his bride—tanned rabbit skin, large enough to sew for mittens or slippers. The snow dampened all sound except the wind. Bear Paw concentrated on the snare and cocked his arm, awaiting the victim.

A sharp rock whistled over Big Bear and struck Bear Paw on the brow. He fell toward his father and collapsed on the fresh snow. Blood gushed from the wound and dyed the snow a brilliant red, even in fading light. Big Bear lifted his son's shoulders and dragged him between two fallen logs. A party of three renegades, distracted by the cache of buffalo meat and folded hide bound to the travois, quarreled over the spoils. Big Bear carried his son from the cove of logs toward the river. Snow fell in clumps and softened the ridges of his footprints.

Big Bear knew the custom of renegade bands: scalping their victims and brandishing the spoils to gain stature. He knew he could not outfight three men. His son's body was relaxed and lifeless. He crept blindly through the snow, along the river in the direction of the village until he reached a point on the shore that abutted an island. He lowered his son's body in the reeds and righted the broken cattails in his path.

The snow fell. No moon shone. Big Bear heard a dry branch snap. The renegade band had begun the search for their victim. Big Bear could escape their attention and return to the village alone, but he couldn't carry his lifeless son. He heard another twig snap farther down the bank. The renegades were circling and returning.

Big Bear leaned over his son, inhaled his spirit and breathed his blessing into the lifeless body. He dragged his son to open water on the far side of the island and eased him into the stream. The body hesitated, then began a slow float away, gliding with ice floes. Before it disappeared, it was covered with snow, at one with the river making its way to the fast current, past the village where the river turns toward the Bright Star, past the bend, flowing, forever flowing to his grave.

WOMEN

The siren atop the fire station startled Mike as he sat in the waiting room of the funeral home. He checked his watch. Six o'clock. If he listened, if he concentrated, he would hear Coach blow the whistle in the college gym and see his buddies fire off one last shot, then rush to mid-court, balls bouncing below the basket.

The momentary diversion was a relief, but now it was back to business. Dad was dead. Dead. Dead. Dead. If he repeated the word, it might lose its power. Dead. Dead. Dead.

Megan his fiancé stood behind him, her thumbs massaging his neck, his shoulders, his back. Mike sat stoic, checked his watch again, and stared at a rack of pamphlets. The table lamps in the waiting room glowed a soft pink, barely illuminating the pamphlet titles. *Alleluia, He Is Risen; Beloved Memories; Sacred Moments.* Mike stood and threw his gloves against the rack. "Bullshit."

Megan picked up the gloves and placed them on the coatrack. She stared at Mike, searching for something to say, something neutral to say. "Anne should arrive soon," she said. "How is she taking it?"

Mike walked to the door of the chapel where Jeff lay in his casket. "Ask her."

"Still in a state of shock, I suspect," Megan said. "Like the rest of us. A bride a couple months ago. A widow today."

Soft organ music whispered out of wall speakers. A coffee maker in the adjoining kitchen gurgled an asynchronous tempo, its aroma a welcome relief from the vapid air of the waiting room.

"Does this change your plans?" Megan asked, still trying for distracting conversation. "Still off to grad school this fall?"

Mike shook his head. "I can't think that far ahead. I have to get through today first. This damned visitation. Then tomorrow. The funeral. The burial. The god-damned luncheon."

Megan walked behind him, wrapped her arms around his waist,

and laid her head on his back. "Easy, big guy," she said. "If you're uncomfortable going home tonight, you can stay at our place. Dad asked me to invite you."

"I'm okay at home. And I want to keep an eye on Anne. None of her family around for hundreds of miles. Made a few friends here, but no support system."

"I'll keep an eye on her too," Megan said. "I like Anne. I like her better than you-know-who."

"Let's keep Mom out of this." Mike checked his watch again. "Neighbors should be showing up soon. I'd better freshen up a bit." He walked to the lobby door.

In the men's room, he looked in the mirror. *Damn. Dump the morbid expression. You look like a snot-faced kid.* He splashed cold water on his face and combed his hair, then pushed his shoulders back. *Stand tall, or those church ladies will hug you to death.*

When he returned to the waiting room, Megan chatted with Anne, both women dressed in black: Megan in a short jacket, jeans, and boots; Anne in a long coat and pantsuit. Mike walked to her, his arms open offering a hug. She held a glob of wet tissues and, with a surprised look, took a reluctant step into his arms. He felt her tremble, then sniffle and stand back. "We're in this together," she said. "Where the hell do they keep the Kleenex?"

"How was Buck?" Mike asked. "Still whimpering?"

"Walks from room to room. Knows something's wrong. Hasn't eaten all day."

"I'll take him for a walk tonight," Mike said.

Anne reached for his arm. "I'll join you."

Mike walked to the waiting room window. Headlights cut through the darkness and proceeded to a parking spot by the door. "Here they come," Mike said. He led the way into the chapel where the director arranged baskets of flowers beside the casket. The organ music followed them in. The air was cooler. Colder.

"Don't worry about the temperature," the director said. "When this place fills up, you'll wish you had air conditioning." He walked to open the double doors to the lobby. "Come in," he said to a woman signing the guest register.

The woman stuffed a prayer card in her pocket of her ersatz leopard-skin jacket and staggered toward Mike. "Hello, stranger," she said, smoothing her disheveled hair.

"Mom. What the hell are you doing here?"

She stopped and pointed to her chest. "Me? Your mom? Am I not invited? Married to the guy for twenty-some years and not invited?"

Mike turned toward the casket, then back. "I'm surprised, that's all." He held a hand out to shake hers. "You remember Megan. And this is Anne."

"Happy to meet you, Anne. I'm Kim. Quick marriage for you, huh? Barely past the honeymoon and wham-oo. Widowhood."

Anne stammered. "Well . . . yes. Would you like coffee?"

"What I'd like is to have a talk with you two. If not tonight, tomorrow. Did Jeff leave a will? Have you talked to his attorney?"

"Mom. Not here. Not now." Mike grabbed her arm and headed for the director's office.

She shrugged him off. "You know I don't beat around the bush, Mikey." She approached him, her breathy words reeking of peppermint. "I'm not standing idly by and let this woman," she pointed at Anne, "inherit his estate. I gave him twenty years. She gave him what? Twenty days?"

"Mom. For Christ's sake." He scanned the room. No neighbors had arrived. "Shut up."

"Don't talk to your mother that way, Mikey. You want me to roll over and play dead? That estate is part mine, and I'll fight to get it. I've already talked to my attorney. He suggested reopening the divorce settlement."

"Mom, you're drunk or you're high or you're on something. Don't you know why you and Dad split? Give it up."

"I know why Jeff and I split," Kim hissed. "You. You forced your way between us. Told him lies about me. Forced him to make a choice. 'Either she goes or I go,' you said. Well, I left, but guess what? I'm back."

Mike dropped his shoulders and turned to Megan. He stood speechless.

Megan stepped forward, faced Kim, and grabbed her sleeve. "Let's step in the director's office and talk."

Kim pulled away. "What I have to say I want to say in front of her. And him." She pointed to the casket.

"All right," Megan said. "First you'll listen to me. You screwed up. You asked for the divorce. You got your half. More than your half.

Way more than you deserved. Then you blew it, right? In a year, you spent half of what he earned in a lifetime." She stared at Kim. "Now you want his half? What kind of leech are you?"

"Stay out of this, girlie," Kim shouted. "And shut up. This is between Mike and me and her."

"Sorry, Kim." Megan poked her shoulder. "You're dealing with me now. Did you tell your attorney how you blew your divorce settlement? Don't you know everybody in town knows you're messing around with anybody in sight? Do you think any judge would be sympathetic to your story? Never. Save yourself the embarrassment. Get a life. And get the hell out of here."

Kim looked at Anne. Anne looked at Megan. Megan looked at Mike. Mike looked at the casket. He did a double-take. Was that grin always there?

TRAFFIC JAM

*C*lick click click. Sam's ring finger drums the steering wheel. He eyes the clock. Six forty-seven. Traffic has jammed for an hour. His mother-in-law's flight is due in five minutes. He taps the radio on, then taps it off. Ahead, to his right, brake lights define the freeway as a miles-long dotted red line. To his left, more brake lights stretch out and shimmer in waves of pavement heat. Straight ahead, a squat trailer waits, loaded with watermelons and bearing Iowa license plates.

The trailer's rear bumper is papered with stickers. *What would Jesus do? When guns are outlawed, only outlaws will have guns. How's my driving? Call 1-800 EAT SHIT.* And near the bottom, *Honk if you love Jesus.*

Click click click. What the hell. *Honk honk honk.*

The woman driver to Sam's right shoots him a stern glance. He points to the bumper sticker, smiles, and honks again. She smiles and taps her horn.

On his left, a van from Good Samaritan waits, its passengers' noses pressed flat against the windows, their eyes straining to focus.

Sam rolls his window down. "Do you love Jesus?" *Honk honk honk.* They grin, then wiggle in their seats like puppets. The van driver honks.

Ahead, the door of the Iowa truck opens. The driver bounces to the pavement. He's short, wears a black muscle T-shirt and denim cutoffs. Body hair peeks from under his shirt and mats his neck and shoulders. He walks to the rear of his truck, to the source of the honking. His slouched gait lowers his left hand to the pavement. In his right, he holds a Coke.

"What the Sam Hill's all the damn racket?"

More cars honk.

"We love Jesus," Sam says. *Honk honk honk.*

The truck driver peers beneath a bushy brow and swivels his head. A chorus of honks echoes up and down the freeway.

THAT REMINDS ME

Sam checks his watch. The plane should be landing now. He's frustrated, angry, furious. He opens the car door and springs out. He's hot. He rips his shirt off and waves it over his head. The woman to his right climbs out and waves a shopping bag. Residents of Good Samaritan open the windows and wave Happy Meal boxes. The truck driver bounces back to his cab.

Above the din, a helicopter hums and chop-chop-chops the air. Channel 5 News. More drivers and passengers empty onto the pavement as the 'copter circles. More shirts and blouses and newspapers wave. Sam remembers a can of spray paint in the trunk. He grabs it and steps from his bumper onto the hood and paints *WE LOVE JESUS* on top of his car. He waves his shirt, careful not to expose his face to the 'copter's camera. Sam glances ahead, sees brake lights release and cars move.

That night as Sam's family watches Channel 5 news, the freeway multi-car accident and traffic jam is the lead story, which segues into the demonstration a couple miles west.

"I think it's wonderful," Sam's mother-in-law says. "Freedom of religious expression is so important."

"You're right," Sam says as the program breaks for a commercial: *New and improved Pine-Sol, an all-purpose household cleaner from a name you trust.* Sam wonders if it removes spray paint.

COMING HOME

Early Sunday morning, and LeRoy stands in the driveway of the old home place wondering who lives there, whether they're awake, whether they're home. The place feels occupied—yard mowed, siding painted, the driveway to the barn graded and tire-worn. No overalls or aprons or diapers on the clotheslines to suggest man, woman, or child inside.

The mailbox is rusted, the printed name indistinct. Gold dandelions surround the milk can that supports it. He remembers that. A late spring sun peeks over the hayfield, sparkling the morning dew. Air is fresh and un-breathed. The heady aroma of mowed hay rides a gentle breeze. He pulls a stem of grass and tastes familiar country.

It's Sunday morning quiet. Mourning doves coo from telephone wires. Then the faint hum of a truck downshifting on the highway a mile north. Back when, Dad would be out of bed climbing into his bibs, Mom in the kitchen brewing coffee, kids feigning sleep until the yell, *Rise and shine.* Holsteins would mill around the barn door or straggle down the lane. Shep would lie on the concrete stoop, head buried under a paw. What felt plain and homely then feels pleasant and desirable now.

Back then, this huge space, this immense arc from horizon to horizon, rendered him tiny and insignificant. Weeks, months, years passed, and he stayed small, a nothing. The cows, the horses, the dog. The milking, haying, barn cleaning, cultivating, fencing. Where were the clothes, the cars, the movies, the weekend flings? Where were the women? Not here.

He remembers riding the milk truck down this driveway to town, satchel in hand, hitching a ride to the city. Not wanting to make a fortune, wanting only to escape.

Now he's back. His family moved years ago. He doesn't flatter himself to think they couldn't make it without him. Dad wouldn't admit that. Mom wouldn't lay the guilt on him.

He picks a few dandelions and inserts them behind the mailbox flag, then stares at the house. A figure appears in the kitchen window. He manages a slight wave, wondering and yearning. Wondering if he should drive in, and yearning for another chance—a chance to love this place as he remembers it, as he loves it now, standing in footprints he created a lifetime ago.

*

Early Sunday morning, and Claire stands at the kitchen window peering over the top of half-curtains looking for intruders. The window is ajar, and a May breeze flutters the curtains against her faded nightgown. This is her morning ritual, although she sees the same landscape every day—no intruders, just the old dairy barn with its sagging spine, the perennial flower garden, the rutted driveway with islands of grass. Better safe than sorry, she says. Who knows what derelict would find her, an aging widow, easy prey?

She turns to the garden and catches her breath. The first peony, an extravagant rose color, has burst into bloom overnight. She won't pick flowers for a bouquet. They're lovelier in the garden, as her mother would . . . What's that at the end of the driveway? A man leaning against the mailbox, his car idling beside him. She hears the purr of the engine.

Who is he and what does he want? She slides the curtain panels together and glances down at her near-naked body. She backs away from the window and combs fingers through her tousled hair. Should she make coffee? Should she get dressed? Should she unlock the door or keep it locked?

With one finger, she pushes bifocals up the bridge of her nose and peeks over the curtains.

A young man, she decides, from his shock of sandy hair. Average height and build. Well-dressed. He's waving. Oh, my God, could it be Robby? He's been gone twelve years and was eighteen when he ran away and joined the Army. The stranger could be thirty. Could be Robby's size at thirty.

Oh, my God. Get something decent on. She runs to the bedroom and slides a dress over her nightgown, then stops at the bathroom to brush her hair. Robby. What if it's Robby? She knew he'd

142

come back. Someday, he'd return. She races to the door.

As she opens it, the car pulls away. She freezes, then scurries down the driveway waving her arms. Robby, Robby. The car accelerates and disappears around a curve.

Robby, she whimpers. You'll be back, won't you Robby? Now that you know where I live. How did you find me? And the man who tormented you, who tormented me—how did you know he passed?

She turns and stumbles toward the house. It was too early for him to stop, she reasons. Too early to drive in, to knock on her door. But he'll be back later this morning. There's time to bake cinnamon rolls. Oh, how Robby loved fresh, hot cinnamon rolls loaded with raisins and smothered with sugar frosting.

She glances at the garden, then walks to the blooming peony. She buries her face in its soft silky petals and picks it, then returns to the kitchen to reach for the crystal vase, a wedding present, in the upper cupboard.

ARC OF INNOCENCE

She looked familiar, the tall, attractive artist in the gallery wearing teal blue that rushed the winter season into spring. She chatted with a customer beside a framed painting on an easel. Who was she? If he walked by, maybe he could glimpse her signature, her name. He approached the artist, hands in pockets, his head tilted up as if viewing the top tier of the gallery. He feigned an interest in a painting behind the easel and stooped to view it, then glanced aside. *Featured Artist Sheryl Harper Henke.* He stood, pinched his chin, then continued his casual stroll.

From the opposite side of the gallery, he watched the artist. Might that be Sheryl Harper, the student he knew forty, fifty years ago? The student who lived across the hall in the apartment house off campus. The blond girl who said hello and smiled when they met, who brought his mail upstairs and slid it under his door. Who met him in the entry one rainy April evening and talked of a busy shift at her part-time waitress job. Was he busy tonight? he recalled her asking. Would he give her a massage?

At the easel, she turned, and when their eyes met, he looked away.

It could be Sheryl. Tall. Attractive. Right age. Blond hair gone to silver. And the artistic bent. She had been an art major.

For the moment, he was alone. His daughter Jenna was in the loft, sorting through a box of prints, something for the cabin kitchen. Or maybe something for her mother, his wife, who didn't join the Grand Marais outing and spent the weekend at her new home, Good Shepherd Assisted Living.

"What do you think of these?" Jenna walked toward him holding a trio of flower prints. "And did you see the painting beside the artist? Maybe something for Mother."

He scanned the prints.

"I miss Mother," Jenna said. "I wish she were here."

"Seems strange without her, doesn't it? But it's a relief not to worry about her tripping on rocks or being overexposed to lake chill. Let's enjoy the weekend." He shrugged his shoulders. "I'm overdosed on culture, Jenna. I'll step outside and enjoy the lake air. Take your time."

He stood on the porch of the gallery, snugged his collar tight, and inhaled the crystalline Lake Superior air. Wind gusts hustled whitecaps on the harbor; a few sailboats bobbed at anchor. Gulls squawked and circled the parking area, scrambling for a half-eaten sandwich. The town felt chilled and vacant. He fought the urge to turn, to look inside the gallery toward the artist. Another urge to think of his invalid wife.

He and Sheryl had never been more than housemates. No love affair, no relationship, no dating he could recall. Nothing, except one night. He leaned on a porch post and closed his eyes. The flattering shock of her request that night, and the boldness of her initiative. His quick shower. Rehearsing what he'd say, when he'd say it. A dim light from a closet door left ajar. Getz/Gilberto on the stereo. Wine glasses and a bottle of Chianti. The interminable wait from the moment she mentioned the massage until her knock on the door.

And then . . . no calculation, no reasoning, no debating morality, no consideration of consequences. For an instant, time stopped. Years of anticipation—the locker room brag sessions, the sneaked book passages, the X-rated films, all materialized. For an instant, everything was corporeal and visceral. Everything was colossal and climactic.

And then?

Days and weeks following, he avoided her in the hall, parked his car out of sight, stuffed a towel under the door to hide the light.

They crossed paths at times, always friendly, always strained. At graduation, she approached him as he stood with his family. "We made it," she said. He offered her a clumsy handshake, then wondered why. His indifference embarrassed him then. It conflicted him now.

Jenna interrupted his reverie. "Dad, I love that artist's painting." She took his arm. "I think Mom would like it. Actually, it might cheer her up."

"Yes, she would like it."

"I talked to the artist. Sheryl something."

"Sheryl Harper something."

"You know her?"

"I'm not certain."

"She said you looked familiar. She asked my name, asked if I was related to you."

A gust of wind blew mist off the harbor, flapping a string of black and white pennants that clung to the porch railing. He turned toward the harbor, the lake, the interminable expanse of water and sky.

"I asked her to join us for lunch at noon. She recommended The Angry Trout. We can walk it."

He stared at the invisible horizon, mulling where sky and water intersected, marveling over their seamless transition. "How do they do it?"

"Do what, Dad?"

"The lake. The sky. How do they become one?"

"You're hallucinating, Dad, which means you're hungry. Let's go."

They walked in silence, the sidewalk empty. She hugged his arm. "I have a feeling there's something I don't know. Care to comment?"

"No." They walked past stores lingering in post-winter dormancy, shop doors signed *Open Soon*.

"You might want to talk, Dad, because my imagination will contrive a juicier scenario than the one you're hiding. Let me guess. I have unidentified siblings. You and Sheryl were busted in a drug raid. I'm adopted, and I have now met my birth mother."

"No, no, and no."

"If not that, what?"

He opened the door of The Angry Trout. A Mozart symphony floated in the air, along with the aroma of butter-sautéed salmon. "Three for lunch," he said to the hostess. "And a table by the window, please."

He sat, unfolded and folded his napkin, opened and closed the menu, clasped his hands. He looked at the harbor, looked at Jenna.

"Worse than what I speculated?" Jenna asked.

"No, it's clumsy, that's all. Talking about indiscretions with your kids is clumsy. Truth is, it was a one-night stand when we were in college."

"And you feel clumsy about that? I'm happy you had a normal adolescence. Tell me there's more."

"No more. No more questions. No more answers. Case closed."

He glanced at the door. "There's Sheryl." He waved and beckoned her to the table.

"Tell me about the painting." Jenna leaned toward Sheryl as she sat. "I can't wait to tell Mom. What inspired it? Does it have a name?"

"It's called *Arc of Innocence*. What inspired it? Life, I guess."

"But it's a happy picture. Bright colors. Symmetrical design. Soft curved shapes. *Arc* denotes something transitioning from one extreme to another. Innocence to what? Guilt?"

"The journey of innocence needn't lead to guilt. It may lead to growth, to empathy, to deeper understanding of one's self." Sheryl delivered the words as if she had spoken them dozens of times. "We're born to lose our innocence. It's only a matter of time."

Jenna glanced at her dad, then pulled away from the table. "Excuse me, Sheryl. I'll step out and call Mom. Order me a bowl of clam chowder, Dad." She walked outside and circled the sidewalk.

"So, how have you been, Garrett? It's been years."

He watched his daughter through the window, phone to her ear, pacing, gesturing.

"Don't be afraid, Garrett. I won't hurt you."

He met her gaze. "You look great. And you've done well with your art." He pointed to Jenna. "You've made one more person happy."

"And you, Garrett. I understand you've also done well. Pardon my curiosity, but is there a health issue with your wife?"

"We transferred her to an assisted living home last week. Beautiful place, but the art is appalling. How much Thomas Kinkade must we tolerate? Jenna is excited about your painting."

The waitress filled water glasses and took their orders.

"And you, Sheryl. You left Minnesota to practice your art?'

"California. Years ago. Once when I returned, I visited the campus. I drove by our apartment house, which is now a parking lot. I felt an urge to look you up."

"That would have been easy. I'm in the phone book."

"Yes, and so is your law firm. I searched your name and learned of your wife Eleanor, your daughters Ellie and Jenna, your prominent cases, your professional awards and appointments. It seemed you led a perfect life. Why disturb it?"

"What prompted the urge?"

Sheryl rotated her water glass, her eyes sinking into the eddy.

148

"I've always felt guilty about that night. How brazen of me to throw myself at you. I can't deny that it was premeditated. I planned it for weeks. Spring semester was nearly over. Who knew where we'd be next year?"

"I didn't consider it brazen."

"Any woman would have." She raised her eyes to meet his. "I had this god-awful crush on you."

He breathed deep and smiled. "Ironic, isn't it, how we delete the little, unpleasant events of life from memory. But the events we remember are the hurtful ones, the regretful ones. Often at the hands of someone we love and respect." He reached his hands across the table to touch hers. "If you were asking for forgiveness, you have it."

She touched his fingers.

"One disclaimer," he said. "I remember avoiding you after that night. Out of shame? Out of embarrassment? Out of fear? I don't know." He swallowed. "Maybe out of fear of inadequacy. Fear of inexperience."

"No, no," she said and squeezed his hand. "I never felt that."

"For your information, I've carried guilt around too." He returned the squeeze. "I remember the feeling that night. The out-of-the-park home run. The center court shot that beat the buzzer. The wanting to, the *having* to tell someone. But no one to tell."

"I know," she said. "Then, the next day, you hear someone sing, 'Is that all there is?' and you know what they're singing about."

"I will confess to a slight case of bewilderment at the time." He sat back in his chair and relaxed his shoulders. "I wondered for a while . . . I wondered days later if . . ."

"You wondered if I was pregnant?"

"Yes."

"Honest?"

"Yes."

"Were you worried or concerned?"

"Both, I suppose."

She pulled her hands from his. "You wondered if I was pregnant, and waited forty years to ask?"

He looked around the café, hoping they were out of hearing distance. He looked outside where Jenna continued gesturing. "I assumed, I concluded that since I didn't hear from you, there was no problem."

"Did you guess I was pregnant?"

He gripped the table. "I don't play guessing games." He glared at her, then relaxed his grip. "Wait," he said. "Ten minutes ago, you saw this meeting as a chance to put a nagging memory to rest. The same for me. Now we're arguing about something that didn't happen." He felt a grin coming. "At least we were smart enough not to pursue a relationship."

She laughed. "I'm not certain of that. It might have been fun."

Jenna walked into the café. "Mother is excited to see the painting. She asked if we'd cut our weekend short and bring it to her, maybe leave after lunch."

He looked at Sheryl, then Jenna. "I have a better idea. You drive down and deliver the painting. Leave me up here to open the cabin. I'll buy supplies in town today, and you can drop me off at the lake."

Jenna hesitated.

"Come back tomorrow or the next day," he said. "I can make it."

"You're okay with that?"

"It was my idea, wasn't it?"

"I'll call Mom and tell her to expect me. Pardon my rudeness again, Sheryl. I'm not good at containing my excitement." Jenna walked to the door.

"I have the last laugh," Sheryl said. "Every time you look at the painting, you'll think of me. I can forget you for another forty years."

"Objection, your honor," he said, reaching for her hands. "There's heavy lifting to do at the cabin." He grinned. "I may need a massage."

She turned to the window to see Jenna walk to the gallery.

He turned and, in the glass, he saw his image, old and respected, yet needful. He saw the muted image of a younger Sheryl—a blond, smiling woman, a woman accompanying him on an earlier adventure, a woman wearing teal blue that reflected spring on bare gray shrubbery outside.

I HAVEN'T THOUGHT OF HER

"My name is Dennis, and I'm a mild schizophrenic."

"You're minimizing, but welcome to the group, Dennis."

"Group? It's just you and me."

"The others will straggle in. Kirk often has to work overtime. Lynn has babysitting problems. Alvina always get stuck in traffic. We'll start without them."

They sat in a church basement under a picture of Jesus surrounded by curly-haired Jewish kids in L.L.Bean robes and funky sandals. On the blackboard in fine Palmer penmanship was scripted *Jesus Saves.* Below it, erased but legible, *Moses Invests.* And below that, in bold print *X-Gens Spend.*

"So, what brings you to our group, Dennis?" The facilitator, on the down side of forty, wore a Donald Trump comb-over. A toothpick wiggled on his lip like a metronome. He wore cargo shorts and a gray sweatshirt emblazoned *Rehab is for Quitters.* His sandals resembled those in the Jesus picture.

"My insurance no longer covers psychiatric care," Dennis said. "My therapist suggested a group."

"Welcome. But you're here for more than the pleasure of our company, right?"

"I have issues." Dennis gulped a Mountain Dew that had warmed between his knees. "I was working on one issue that intrigued my therapist—my search for something to believe in. All my life, I've been surrounded by people who deal in hard provable facts. Dad was an insurance actuary. He had more faith in statistical sampling than most people have in God. Mom was a high school math teacher. She looked at me one day, perplexed, and said, 'Honey, if you were a quadratic equation, I could solve you.'" Dennis lowered his head. "My sisters were just as bad. Worse."

"You wanted to believe in something?" the facilitator asked.

"Yeah. Yeah. I wanted the mystery, the *esoterica*, the profundity of accepting truth on its word. To make the quantum leap from ignorance to acceptance by faith, not by facts." He heaved a breath and sipped his Mountain Dew. The facilitator looked at his watch.

"I remember the Christmas my sister informed me that Santa Claus was a myth," Dennis said. "Something parents invented to coerce kids into good behavior during Christmas vacation. That, and an opportunity for Target to sell toys and toasters. On Christmas Eve, my sister showed me the sales receipt for my Lego Building Blocks. My gift from Santa was from Toys"R"Us. Then she sneered, 'I can be as naughty as I want, and I'll still get a sweater.'"

"How did that make you feel?"

"How did that make me feel? Not so good, I guess."

"So your older sister debunked the Santa Claus myth. What else?"

Dennis noticed the facilitator taking notes. "I loved the Adam and Eve story. The Garden of Eden. Year 'round summer. Walking naked in a lush garden with a long-haired blond. No mosquitoes, no lawn to mow, no snow to shovel. Then, in high school we learned the theory of evolution. Turns out we're all slime, snails, chimps. I couldn't buy it.

"I remember stating my case for creationism at a family picnic, my aunts and uncles smiling their patronizing smiles. 'That's pretty profound for a high school kid,' Uncle Roy said. 'Let's see. Adam and Eve had Cain and Abel and some other kids. Cain killed Abel, but somebody had to procreate the species. Just brothers and sisters. Hmmm. That explains why we're all a little crazy.' He went goo-goo-eyed and shook like he was having a seizure. He set his beer can on his crotch and spilled all over his pants. 'Hey, sis,' he yelled, 'come here.' The family went hysterical. I broke into tears and ran." Dennis sipped on an empty can.

Carillon bells chimed the quarter hour. The facilitator combed fingers through his hair. He lifted a sandaled foot and placed it on his tanned knee, his little toe adorned with a silver ring. "I'm sure there were other disappointments for you," he said. "The Easter Bunny. The Great Pumpkin. Snow White."

"All of those," Dennis said. "My belief system came tumbling down like the Berlin Wall. In college, we were guaranteed an A in philosophy if we denied the existence of God. Actually I preferred

Spinoza's interpretation of a higher power over the white-robed, omniscient Father figure who rules from up there." He pointed to the ceiling where foil stars were pasted around painted clouds, opened to reveal angry eyes.

The facilitator looked at his watch. "Kirk or Lynn or Alvina should be walking in any minute. So, did those revelations anger you? Enlighten you? Liberate you? Did you argue your case or tuck your tail between your legs?"

"I didn't lose sight of my quest, my search for something to believe in. The woods were full of college girls back then. Lustful and lewd girls. They wore their promiscuity like charm bracelets, a charm for every guy they did that semester. One wore a sweatshirt that said, *To err is human, to rut divine.*

"I still believed that for every man there was a woman. My challenge was to find her. I wanted to believe in true love. The Perfect Marriage. *Until death do us part,* and all that crap. Like Jessica Tandy and Hume Cronyn, Edward Hopper and Georgia O'Keefe, Roslyn and Jimmy Carter. These are talented people, intelligent, successful, who could have anyone they wanted. But they remained true. Usually."

The door opened, and a man about Dennis's age walked in. He had troll-doll green hair and wore a T-shirt with the inscription *Ask me about my member.* Dennis looked down at the unused commercial real estate on his own shirt.

"Who's the new kid?" the man asked.

"Kirk meet Dennis. Dennis, Kirk."

Dennis offered his hand which held the crushed Mountain Dew can.

"We were talking about Dennis's quest, Kirk. May I summarize for you, Dennis?" He nodded at Dennis but didn't wait for a response. "His Holy Grail is to find something not to know but to believe. We're up to true love."

"Bullshit," Kirk said. An unlit cigarette butt dangled from his lip like a loose tooth.

"I thought it was possible," Dennis ignored the interruption, "because it happens in animals. Swans mate for life. Doves mate for life. Then I read a study where DNA from a set of hatchlings was compared. Guess what? Different dads. Can you imagine a mother swan screwing around? A mother dove? A mother chickadee?"

THAT REMINDS ME

"That's helpful," Kirk said.

"Talk about your progress toward finding true love, Dennis," the facilitator said. He spit out a chewed toothpick and replaced it.

"I recently split with Margaret Mary." Dennis bit his lip and looked at his shoes, which were rocking. He sighed. "I haven't thought of her for days. We had a disagreement. No, an argument." He looked up at angry eyes in the ceiling. "No, we had a fight. I said orgasms were overrated. 'What?' she said, 'They're Beethoven's Ninth and hot fudge sundaes and Hawaiian sunsets all rolled into one.'

"'They're overrated,' I repeated. 'You're kidding,' she said, and looked at me with her X-ray, her X-rated eyes. 'Orgasms are an emotional roller coaster,' she said. 'K-chunk, k-chunk, k-chunk all the way to the top. And then? Freefall.' I gave her my best Woody Allen psychotic grin. 'If they're so hot, why do you fake them?'"

Dennis reached and tugged an imaginary cord. "Curtain."

"Is this Margaret Mary chick still on the street?" Kirk asked.

"To the best of my carnal knowledge," Dennis replied.

"Kirk, how was your week?" the facilitator asked.

"Like first day of kindergarten compared to this dude. Are you currently molesting anyone, Dennis?"

Dennis looked at Kirk, then at the facilitator. "This is not what I expected of a group. I'm doing all the talking and it sounds like part confession, part *Desperate Housewives*."

"How does that make you feel?" the facilitator asked.

"Shitty."

"Good. We're making progress. Now, are you currently seeing . . ."

"Not seeing anyone currently, but the last one was Barbara Ann. I think. I haven't thought of her for weeks. I seem to prefer women with two first names. Margaret Mary, Sue Ellen, Jo Lynn, etc. Barbara Ann was a math teacher. Was I looking for my mother? Maybe. She was a strict disciplinarian. In my fantasies, I see her in black latex, black boots, and a collection of paddles—small, medium, large. Extra-large. Huge." Dennis took a deep breath and inhaled dank basement air. "Where was I going with that?"

"Barbara Ann," the facilitator read from his notes.

"Oh, yes. She treated me like a student, not a lover. Insisted on correcting me, coaching me, complimenting me on my day-to-day progress."

"Did you tell her how that made you feel?" the facilitator asked.

"She was indifferent to my feelings. I challenged her on that. I said, 'You know, indifference is an acquired trait.' 'So is sarcasm,' she said. 'I guess it's all over but the shouting,' I said. She snapped, 'It's all over but the pouting.'"

"Is this chick back on the market?" Kirk asked.

"Not officially. I still owe her fifty bucks."

"Bummer," snorted Kirk.

"I think we get the drift," the facilitator said. "Presumably you have reason to believe that this ideal mating scheme is achievable, at something less than celebrity level. Have you actually met an ordinary couple who realized your fantasy? Your parents, for example?"

"Lord, no," Dennis snapped. "Mom and Dad were estranged when she died. I haven't thought of her for months. I remember sitting by her bedside during her final hours at the nursing home. She had a room with a garden view and a birdfeeder. Doves, chickadees, no swans. On her wall was a cross-stitched sampler that read *Give us this day our daily prunes.*

"She knew the score, knew she was going to die. I asked her if she had any unfinished business that I could wrap up for her. Like a kind word of forgiveness for Dad."

Dennis heaved a sigh and tossed the Mountain Dew can in the wastebasket. "'Nothing,' she said, so I asked her if she had any regrets, like treating Dad like a stray cur. 'Just one,' she said. I sidled close to her and held her trembling hand. The skin on her arm looked like a sepia map of Europe. Her voice was confident, her breathing labored.

"'What was your one regret?' I whispered. She lifted her eyes to the ceiling and I think she saw the same pair of eyes I see. 'I regret that I never was a contestant on Queen for a Day.'

"'Queen for a Day. What's that?' 'It was a reality quiz show in the sixties,' she announced. 'I can still hear Jack Bailey asking *Would you like to be Queen for a Day?* and the audience screaming and waving their arms like a body possessed. The lucky lady, The Queen, was draped in red velvet and crowned with jewels and carried a dozen long-stemmed roses. Then they wheeled out her prizes—kitchen appliances, a new wardrobe, bicycles for the kids.' She coughed and asked for a sip of water.

"I moved closer to her and whispered in her ear in a voice that I hoped would sound like Jack Bailey. 'Would you like to be Queen for a Day?' She jerked her hand from mine and waved her arms and shouted Yes, yes. She choked, grabbed her chest, and rolled her eyes into her forehead. And she expired."

"Subscriptions expire," Kirk said. "People die."

"I'm sorry," the facilitator said.

"I think I got it." Kirk grinned like he had solved the riddle of life. "You feel responsible for your mother's death. This true love crusade is a sham."

"Why do I feel I'm not supposed to be here?" Dennis asked. "Why don't we let Kirk talk?"

"Because it's easier learning from your mistakes than making my own," Kirk said.

"Let's get back on track," the facilitator said. "So you continued searching for true love. You weren't successful finding it for yourself. You must have known it could exist outside New York City or Hollywood. A Minnesota couple to direct you, beacons shining through the fog in our land of 10,000 lakes."

"There was. Dr. Paul Sampson and Dr. Inez Sampson. Both taught at the University. He taught Composition, she taught Literature. Charming couple, in and out of the classroom. They lived in an ivied cottage along Fraternity Row. Climbing roses and garden statuary outside, original art and Persian rugs inside. New York Times best sellers splayed on the coffee table. Students were invited for end-of-the-semester parties. Real honest-to-goodness food, brand name beer, Dave Brubeck. And easy, meaningful chatter."

"Sounds like a *but* coming," the facilitator said. "Let me guess. You detected a flaw in the system, a fly in the ointment."

"A pea under the mattress," Kirk added.

Dennis sniffled and lowered his head. "That summer, Dr. Inez, the Lit professor, was offered a gig at Princeton to teach Chaucer. Some Bloomberg Foundation money to immerse corporate bigwigs into culture. Of course, there were cocktail parties. Of course there were unfettered married men on a two-week fling. Of course there was this charming lady from the Midwest who pronounced her Rs and still had red hair and freckles dotting her neck and chest. And of course, virtue didn't stand a chance in the face of all that money and power and position.

"I looked her up. She still taught at the University. He didn't. I couldn't hide my disappointment when I learned the truth. 'You were my reason for optimism,' I told her. 'Optimism?' she laughed. 'That went out with Candide.'"

"She told you all this?" the facilitator asked.

"Most of it. I connected a few dots. She told me I should look up Paul. Dr. Paul. 'Talk to him,' she said. I called Dr. Paul and asked if he'd meet me for lunch. We sat at an outdoor restaurant in Dinkytown and suffered through the small talk. 'I had a nice visit with Dr. Inez,' I said, and gulped my wine.

"'Inez.' He sounded surprised. 'I haven't thought of her for years.'"

WITNESS

"I'll be glad when this call is over. The Lord is demanding a lot of me today." Jacob checked his watch, then placed a rubber band around an *Awake* and *Watchtower* pamphlet. "Maybe she won't be home."

Isaiah held both hands to the wheel of the old Dodge station wagon and steered it down the gravel road. "She's always been home ever since I started the mission. I think she enjoys challenging us. She mentioned years ago she had a degree in Theology, with a concentration on biblical studies."

"Sometimes I wish I hadn't given up my Watkins route," Jacob said. "Back then, I at least knew my product better than my customers did. They ran to meet me at the car, not lock their doors when they saw me coming."

Isaiah was quiet.

Jacob knew what he was thinking. "You're right. The Lord provided me with a reason to mend my ways. Three accidents in one year. That Watkins vanilla is 8.25 percent alcohol, you know."

"Trust the Lord," Jacob said.

"Maybe she won't want to discuss her version of the Bible today. Maybe she'll be fixing supper. Maybe she'll take pity on us."

"The Lord will ask no more than you can deliver."

"Did you ever wonder if this is your true calling?" Jacob asked. "Selling salvation that no one wants to buy?"

Isaiah glared at him for an instant. He took a deep breath and sighed. "I can't lie. It has crossed my mind. The Devil loves to tempt me. But every time, the Lord rescues me."

"Tempts you? How?"

"Have you ever made calls by yourself? You'd be surprised how many lonely housewives there are out there. Lonely, or have a perverted sense of humor."

Jacob shrugged his shoulders. "Wow."

"Why do you suppose they send us in pairs?"

The sky to the west shone blazing red when they turned in the driveway. A light shone through the window of the house. Smoke swirled from the chimney. A shaggy Newfoundland dog waggled out to meet the car.

"She's home," Isaiah said. He parked in front of the garage and turned off the ignition. Doffing his hat and bowing his head, he folded his hands. "Lord, that we may expand Thy kingdom."

"In His name we pray." Jacob lifted his head and reached for his briefcase. "Let's go."

"Five o'clock, and it's dark already," Jacob said on the walk to the door. "I told Arlene I'd be home by 5:30."

"The Lord's work is our top priority," Isaiah said as he knocked.

Mrs. Hamilton opened the door. "I knew you were coming," she said. "The neighbors have an alert system. Two men in a car, both wearing neckties. How many people up and down the road answered the door?"

"The Lord's word will find a way," Isaiah said, handing her the pamphlets.

"Who is it, Gladys?" A man's voice wheezed from a back room.

"The Jehovah's Witnesses."

"Tell them we don't want any."

"You were here about a month ago and left pamphlets," Mrs. Hamilton said. "I've been waiting to ask you a few questions."

Isaiah leaned forward. Jacob sneaked a look at his watch.

"About *the one true faith*," Mrs. Hamilton said. "You believe that you found it, right?"

"Oh, yes." Isaiah nodded his head. "If mine wasn't the one true faith, I'd search for it."

"But if it's the one true faith for you, is it the one true faith for the rest of the world?"

"Yes, yes. God's truth is universal. It is our mission to bring you the truth."

"You won't run out of prospects then," Mrs. Hamilton said. "You may have a problem convincing all the Jews and Muslims and Hindus and Buddhists, not to mention your fellow Christians. But tell me about the Bible. You interpret it as the absolute word of God, right? Immutable and infallible for all time, correct?"

160

"Yes, the Bible." Isaiah reached in the pocket of his coat and retrieved a small book. He patted it and held it to his heart. "Everything we need to know is here."

"And a few things we don't need to know. Slavery, for example. And human sacrifice. Doesn't the Old Testament condone that?"

Isaiah looked at Jacob. Jacob looked at his hands. "I haven't read the Hebrew text," Isaiah said. "Sometimes passages suffer in translation." He reached into his briefcase. "You might be interested in this." He handed her a copy of *What Does the Bible Really Teach?*

"I'll look at it, but I don't expect to find those answers. Another question. I notice that you are strong believers in Creationism. Doesn't science disprove much of what is written in the Bible? Do you believe in the seven-day creation cycle? Adam and Eve? The Garden of Eden?"

"With all my heart and soul," Isaiah said. "A beautiful story of God's might and beneficence, and man's ingratitude and weakness."

"Do you see it as metaphor or fact?"

"Fact, ma'am. It's all spelled out there in the book." He slid a finger around his shirt collar and felt sweat building under his arms.

"You might be thinking about how your story will play when forms of life are discovered in other galaxies. But enough for today." She smiled. "Excuse me a second."

She walked to the kitchen and returned with a plastic bag of cookies. "Thanks so much for talking to me. Or letting me talk to you. My everyday conversations are limited to 'Did you take your pills?' or 'Should I turn down the heat?' or 'Should I turn up the volume?' I haven't talked ideas for years."

"Charity is its own reward," Isaiah said, reaching for the cookies. "I hope you find answers to your searching in that book. Or the Bible." He opened the door.

Outside, Jacob petted the dog on the walk. "It's times like this I wish I still was a drinking man."

Isaiah wiped his hand across his brow. "We're not that far from the Broken Hart."

TWO BIRDS, ONE STONE

The scene opens in a white-walled hospital room. A woman lies in bed in a white gown connected to life-saving apparatus. She speaks in a struggling voice. A man in a suit stands beside her.

She: What did the doctor say?
He: A week. A month. A year. He doesn't know.
　　He pats her hand and scans the tubes, the wires, the dials.
She: How can anyone allow himself such uncertainty?
He: You have uncommon complications.
She: If they were common, I wouldn't want them.
　　The room is quiet except for ticking of the cardiac monitor.
She: Turn that off. It sounds like a time bomb.
He: We shouldn't turn it off. Would you like a 7-Up? The doctor said carbonation will soothe your stomach.
She: Yes. Anything soothing. Even the simple pleasure of watching bubbles rise in the glass. Bubbles. Until now, I associated bubbles with pleasure. Bubble bath, bubble gum, Bubbles LaRue. Did I tell you about Bubbles LaRue? Many lives ago, but a fun memory.
He: I don't remember her.
She: She was my grad school roommate. Funded her masters by stripping at the Kit Kat Lounge. Oh, the strange men she met, the laughs we had.
　　He fluffs her pillows and straightens the coverlet over her legs.
She: What time is it? Must be time for my medication.
He: It's only seven-thirty. You can't have your pain pill until nine.
She: I can't wait that long. I won't wait that long. This pain . . .
　　He hears conversation in the hall and glances at the door. A doctor and nurse walk by, the doctor dictating, the nurse taking notes.
He: I have a surprise. Remember the Easter lily I bought for you? When I worked the garden, I cut the dead stem and set the bulb in the flower

bed. It grew. And it has three buds. Your Easter lily may bloom in October.

She: Do you expect me to find hope in the metaphor? Easter lily. Rising from the dead?

She motions at the glass, and he lifts the straw to her lips.

She: You planted the lily. The glorious and immortal resurrection is yours.

He: Don't think about that. I don't.

She: Please do. You may have to suffer with me another day, another week. Tell me that if you don't already have plans, you'll make them. Another woman. Another marriage. Another life. But I don't want her to wear my jewelry. Promise?

He: Promise.

She: So you have plans or you don't?

He: It's crossed my mind, but I don't have plans.

She: Plans of what? With whom?

He: You're way ahead of me. The grief counselor said . . .

She: You're seeing a grief counselor?

He: I've had a couple sessions. She said the ill spouse is often heartened to know the other may someday find . . . find new happiness.

The call system at the nurses' station blurts a series of blasts, and the hall scrambles with people running past their door pushing med carts, oxygen, a gurney. More nurses, doctors, orderlies. He closes the door.

She: Someone didn't make it.

The monitor ticks, ticks, ticks.

She: I have a solution.

She touches his hand.

She: The doctor said taking pain killer meds with the nitro could be fatal. It's such a simple solution. An elegant, simple solution. One pill; two lives. Yours to live. Mine to . . ."

He turns from her to the window where Venus glows in the darkening sky.

He: Venus. Lovely and contradictory Venus.

He pulls the drape open.

He: Can you see her?

She: No, no.

He: Venus. Morning star and evening star. Contradictory like hope and despair, life and death.

She: Yes, yes.

MAN OF THE YEAR

This morning, the countryside has an sweetness about it, like a farm photograph on a feed store calendar. Hayfields are manicured green rectangles. Black spruce windbreaks run true east and west. Farmsteads—L-shaped white houses, hip-roofed red barns, green-treed yards—are neat and trim and precise.

This morning, Holsteins amble out the barn door, drink from the stock tank, and wait near the gated lane in pastel morning sun to be driven to pasture.

Pigs root in the shade of the pen. Others lie on their sides in mud, warming to the sun. Sheep graze, unconcerned and unfenced, in tall grass of an abandoned orchard.

This morning, the sun urges moss roses open in vivid pinks and yellows and oranges in the rock garden. Chickens scratch and peck in the dusty driveway. A retired Black Lab sleeps on the granary stoop. Indifferent cats groom themselves in fresh-cut hay stacked on the wagon. A mourning dove coos a baleful cry.

Young Mick plays in the yard while his father Mel Fritz finishes chores in the barn. Mother Lorene referees the school-aged kids in the house, reciting her litany of morning instructions. *Eat your toast. Keep an eye on the clock. Don't forget your lunch money.*

The kids zip from room to room, gathering homework off the piano, yelling for help to find a missing shoe, watching through the kitchen window for the bus. Across the kitchen on a picture wall, framed photographs document early lives of these children—baptisms, first days of school, visits to Santa—and the early lives of their parents —Lorene's nursing school graduation portrait, Mel's picture in U.S. Army uniform, mounted and framed beside a cover of *TIME* magazine, the wedding party.

The school bus rounds the corner of the road. The screen door swings open as kids sprint down the worn dusty driveway. From his seat on the granary step, Mick watches them board the bus and traces a road with a stick in the dirt. A mother hen *cluck clucks* her newly hatched brood to the rotting remains of a haystack. The chicks mimic mother hen, stray from the flock, and are clucked back. Mick watches the yellow babies wander and return, scratch and peck. Mother hen pecks her way to the hay wagon. The cats, groomed and stoic, eye the chicks. An old tom jumps from the wagon and crouches by a tire. The mother hen squawks and screeches, calling the chicks. A rooster joins the melee.

Mick runs for the cat, picks it up, and carries it to the stock tank. The cat hisses and claws at Mick, scratches his arms and face, and jumps to the ground. Mick screams, raises his bleeding arms, and stumbles to the barn.

Mel runs from the barn, stops when he sees the bleeding child, hears the child screaming, the chickens screeching. He freezes. Blood. Screaming. What starts as a slow, high-pitched whistle in his head grows shrill, sharp, deafening. The ground vibrates. The granary rumbles and rocks. Dust rises from the ground and falls from the building. Through the dust comes the smell of smoke. Mel runs blindly for the boy and clutches him.

That morning in 1967, two months before the Tet Offensive, breakfast for Delta Squad was the usual—powdered eggs cooked in a C-ration cup over a C-4 explosive. Sergeant Mel Fritz milled with somber infantrymen around the camp, eating, drinking coffee, smoking. The morning air was menacing, like any day before patrol. A flock of babbler birds screeched a threat high in the canopy of kapok trees. Monkeys bouncing around the periphery of the camp screamed and chattered.

Sergeant Fritz nodded at David Duncan, TIME-LIFE photographer, embedded with Delta Squad. Mr. Duncan enjoyed celebrity status with his battle anecdotes and his daily communication with New York, and home. The squad respected his courage, shooting only his Leica with an unused sidearm for protection.

That morning, Delta Squad patrolled the bombed out Placu region of Vietnam where Allies and Vietcong had seesawed control. They approached a rural village, a moonscape of charred wall studs and metal skeletons surrounded by smoldering ash heaps. Abandoned carts and discarded furniture littered the roadways. A surviving pig scrambled from a pile of rotting garbage at the sight of the advancing infantry.

The Vietcong had fortified themselves and won recent support of the few remaining village inhabitants. The American presence was threatening and intimidating. Children cowered in front of GIs, twice as big as their fathers, who transported an array of hardware from another galaxy. Both the Allies and the Vietcong felt pressure to secure the area around Placu before the monsoons.

That morning, Delta Squad reconnoitered a nearly deserted village near Encau as a base for an offensive into the mountains of the north. According to Military Intelligence, one mountain housed a suspected military base, complete with strategic and tactical headquarters, ammunition depot, and military hospital. Delta Squad had made recon missions through the town, working to gain trust of the few remaining inhabitants, old disabled people and a few children. In time, the children warmed to the GIs and worked their generosity, following them up the pocked trail north of town.

"C-rations? Cigarettes? Gum?" they called.

That morning, Sergeant Mel Fritz stopped to take a radio message from battalion headquarters. "A Vietcong formation is moving down the trail toward your village. Take cover. Do not engage. Then return to base."

The squad scattered in groups of three, Mel's trio finding refuge behind a demolished adobe and pole structure, the remains of a barn. Once settled, they listened for the squawk of jungle birds—parrots, babblers, and parakeets. In the quiet of the village, a rooster crowed, cooking utensils clinked in a makeshift hut, children giggled in an open square. Mel calculated from the bird screeching that he had time to coax the children to safety. A burned bus lay overturned along the road, tires scorched, paint bubbled and peeling, windows shattered. He ran toward the children, motioning them to follow him and, scooping the smallest one in his arm, he headed for the bus. The children thought it a game and followed him. He dumped a pocket of C-rations inside the bus and motioned the children to stay down.

They scampered for the C-rations, and Mel ran for cover, out of distance but in view of the bus. The Vietcong formation was closer now, not visible but within hearing range—the clank of weapons against canteens, the scuffle of boots, whistles that mimicked bird calls. The formation reached the northern edge of the village, creating a cloud of dust as they trampled ruts and pot holes. The platoon leader signaled a halt, and the platoon stopped. Elders of the village retreated to their huts. The children remained hidden in the bus. The pig snorted from the trash pile.

A rifle shot. Two Vietcong soldiers ran to the struggling pig, slit its throat with a bayonet, and carried it by the legs to the platoon leader.

The rifle shot and the shrill squeals of the pig aroused the children. One by one, they stood to look out empty windows at the formation. Two soldiers approached the bus. While one watched the children, rifle ready, the other crawled inside. He backed out, followed by his rifle. On the bayonet was a C-ration bag in an olive drab wrapper with a U.S. stencil. He carried it to the platoon leader who shouted an order and motioned for the formation to proceed. Two Vietcong soldiers stood by as the formation passed through town. When the formation was clear of the bus, one solder jerked a grenade from his belt, pulled the pin, and made an easy lob high in the air. The soldiers ran toward the formation.

The grenade arced high and floated down, striking the side of the bus, rolling along the window ledge. No sound. No sight of the children. The Vietcong formation rounded the bend in a trail of red dust.

A sudden explosion. Dust. Smoke. Steel splintered and rocketed. Sheet metal, torn ragged, soared in jagged chunks. The dust settled, replaced by clouds of acrid black smoke. Leaves trembled down like charred confetti.

Mel ran into the smoke, blinded, not breathing. The smoke thickened as he neared the burning skeleton of the bus. He pulled goggles from his field pack, jerked his helmet aside, and slipped the goggles over his head. The structure of the bus was visible now. Through the smoke, he saw remains of upholstered seat cushions smoldering, silhouetted against a hole torn in the side of the bus. He saw movement under the dashboard in front of the driver's seat—a small child, the one he carried into the bus, crouched in a fetal fold.

The exploding grenade echoed up the valley and aroused the concern of other Delta Squad trios who arrived at the village as Mel ran from the burning bus, carrying the small blackened child out of the smoke. Sergeant Mel, looking otherworldly in his goggles, helmet askew, and a handkerchief tied over his nose and mouth, ran with the child. Photographer Duncan caught the image of terror in the screaming child, the extended arms, the bleeding face.

Mr. Duncan requested that Mel sign a release that night, and he did. The photo made *TIME's* cover when the American GI was designated 1968 Man of the Year.

After the parades, the parties, the reunions; after the newspaper stories, the Sergeant Mel Fritz Commemorative Day; after the nightmares, the drinking sprees, the taming of reflexes; after the wasted separation pay check: after the phone stopped ringing; after the world went back to work, Mel returned to the farm. He married Lorene, and now they have the four kids. His daily routine is predictable—morning chores, field work, evening chores. His seasonal rhythm is gratifying—plow and plant, cultivate and harvest.

This morning, he sits on the ground, leaning against a gnarly box elder tree, sweaty, exhausted, shivering. He dampens his tremors with a confused child hugged in his arms.

Some days his world holds together. Some days it doesn't.

LIAR LIAR

Say what you want about Elaine. Analyze her politics, criticize her decorating, chuckle at her eclectic wardrobe. But this about Elaine you must admit: she throws a helluva party. Her young stylist Daniel will attest. He leans on a kitchen counter sampling a tray of quesadillas and stares through his goblet. "What kind of wine is this?" he asks a white-hatted cook. She lifts a skillet of sautéed onions and peppers, inhales, and flips them. "It sure is tasty," Daniel says to no one.

He was wary of accepting the invitation. "I won't know a soul," he told Elaine.

"You will by the end of the evening. You're coming. Understand?"

The occasion for today's gala is the autumnal equinox, no matter that the event occurred a month ago. "Why now?" a guest asks. Elaine rolls her eyes. "It slipped my mind," she says, and motions to a passing caterer to refill a tray of stuffed jalapeños. Tonight the house and grounds are decorated in a Mexican motif. Woven red, yellow, and green runners adorn the Queen Anne tea tables. Piñatas dangle from columned archways. Huge, gaudy paper flowers bloom in terra cotta urns.

"What's the connection between the autumnal equinox and Mexico?" another guest wonders.

"Doesn't Mexico celebrate the equinox?" she asks. She stands on her toes, tilts her head and drops her chin, and twirls her sarape in a graceful veronica. She smiles. "*Olé.*"

Two Poncho Villa guitar players stroll the foyer, the veranda, the gardens in sequined red sombreros. "Do you know Marty Robbins's 'El Paso'?" a grayed dowager dressed as Miss Havisham asks. Poncho smiles under a black brush of mustache and shakes his head. "*No comprende.*"

Daniel is young for this crowd. He pretends to check his cell phone and turns from the quesadillas to survey the guests. He could be their grandson. They reek of old money, sporting matching toreador outfits or Marie Antoinette and King Louis finery. How could he sneak out without Elaine knowing? A high school student valet had parked his car, God knows where. Might he get a phone call from the shop informing that the plumbing had burst or the electricity failed? No. The shop had closed hours ago. He feels a tap on the shoulder.

"Daniel, come, meet my friends." Elaine tugs at his sleeve. She is an imposing woman, dressed as a flashy Yvonne DeCarlo in a swashbuckler film opposite Stewart Granger.

Daniel resists. "Why do I feel I'm the only one here still wearing braces? And why am I the only one who hasn't been married thirty years?"

"See that woman in the black pantsuit?" Elaine points to a circle of women beside the fireplace. "She hasn't even lived thirty years. Wonderful friend. She's my personal trainer."

Daniel scans the room and lands on the black pantsuit. "You mean the one with her arm around Patty Berg?" He watches her. She seems to be the center of conversation, the other women nodding their heads as she speaks. "She's taller than I am."

"Everyone's taller than you, Daniel. Come. I'll introduce you." Elaine leads the way. "I noticed you were taking a phone call. Problems?"

"The security service called. Seems there's a problem with the locks at the shop. They'll call back." He grabs a fresh wine goblet from a passing caterer.

Elaine wiggles her red ruffled hips in an impromptu conga line through the crowd to the fireplace. "Excuse me, girls. I want to introduce my Daniel. Daniel is new here and eager to make friends, aren't you Daniel?"

Daniel feels a teenaged blush and douses it with a gulp of wine. He nods his head.

"Hi, Daniel. I'm Terry." Black pantsuit reaches to shake his hand, giving it a powerful squeeze. Her caramel brown hair is bobbed, her face sun-tanned, her generous smile showcases an array of pearls. She extends her other hand and cups his. "So pleased to meet you."

Daniel stands on his toes and grinds his teeth to control a pained wince.

"Have you met my friends?" Terry asks. "This is Carla, my

mountain bike buddy."

Carla lunges forward reaching to shake a hand still lost in Terry's grip.

"And this is Sam, my CrossFit training pal. And this is Joey. We ran the Madison Marathon together."

"I whipped her ass too," Joey grunts.

Daniel surveys the group of Amazons. *Why do I feel like Daniel in the lions' den?* he wonders.

"I love your bling, Elaine." Terry reaches for a string of campaign pins that dangle from a silver neck chain. "I love the way it snuggles between Mont Blanc and the Matterhorn. Don't you agree, Daniel?" she asks.

Daniel gulps his wine.

"Who are these people?" Terry asks. She reads the buttons. "Pat Buchanan. Roseanne Barr. Chuck Baldwin. Oh, Ross Perot and Ralph Nader. I recognize them."

"All third party candidates I supported in the past." Elaine jingles the pins.

"My mother had a basset hound named Ross Perot," Joey says.

Daniel fiddles with his watch; Elaine senses his discomfort. "Daniel heard from the security firm that protects his salon. Seems there's a lock problem and he may have to leave for a while. I wanted you to meet him."

"Salon?" Terry raises an eyebrow. "You're a hair stylist?"

Terry winces again at the affected tone of her voice, the implication.

"Yes. And the best one in town." Elaine pats his shoulder. "I'll walk you to the door, Daniel."

Terry reaches to shake his hand, then hugs him. "So glad to meet you, Daniel. I hope to see you again."

Daniel's nose lands on Terry's neck. She presses against him. Her musky perfume, her toned body, her confident aggression tingle his spine, his legs, his toes. Elaine pulls him away. "Adios, girls."

On the way to the door, Elaine locks her arm in Daniel's. "I so wanted you to meet Terry. Isn't she sweet? And so talented." She pauses. "And so unattached. Like someone else I know." She squeezes Daniel's arm.

"She makes a strong first impression. I'm just now getting

feeling back in my hand."

"Would you like to see her again? I could give you her card. Or better yet, come to my Halloween party next month. I'll invite her too."

"Halloween is this month, Elaine."

Elaine shrugs. "You people are so conventional." She kisses Daniel on the cheek. "Watch your mail."

Elaine returns to the guests who have congregated on the veranda where a flamenco guitarist leans into his instrument. A dancer in brilliant orange clicks her castanets, swings her arms, and twirls. Elaine finds Terry. "What do you think?"

"Daniel? Cute. Love that dimpled chin. Is he married?"

"No. Single. Like you."

"And he's never been married? And he's a hair stylist? Makes you wonder. How do you proceed with a guy like that?"

"You're the resourceful one. Figure it out. I invited him to my Halloween party. You come too."

Terry sits on a couch at Elaine's Halloween party. The room glows with lighted jack-o'-lanterns. Arch-backed cats leer from atop a Chippendale armoire. Wispy witches in diaphanous gowns twirl from high ceiling fans. Terry recognizes strains of "Night on Bald Mountain" above the din.

Guests wear outlandish costumes. And masks. The invitation demanded masks, not to be removed until midnight. Daniel wears a blonde Marilyn Monroe wig and pleated white halter dress. And a white lace mask. When he crosses his legs, he sees the shaving nick. He uncrosses them. Terry has haunted him since he met her. He hasn't felt this giddy about a girl since high school. Her confidence—that's what attracts him. That's what he loves. Funny word, *love*. Not in his lexicon. Not until now.

He struggled since meeting her with a plan for tonight. Was she attracted to men? He thought she was, remembering her hug, her clinging to him beyond the prescribed few seconds, her musky fragrance. But she was surrounded by women. Not ultra-feminine women. Might he improve his chances with this getup?

The night wears on. Costumed men ask Daniel to dance. He declines. "Not in these heels." He spots Elaine, regaling the crowd as Scheherazade in rich burgundy satin. A couple in a horse costume graze the hors d'oeuvre table and nibble at a bouquet of orange roses. An

Uncle Sam on stilts hands American flags to disinterested guests. Caterers whisk through the throng, balancing trays of wine glasses. The music volume increases, as does Daniel's fear of failure. Where is Terry? Surely he can spot her, even in disguise.

He scans the room from his vantage point on the couch, wanting a cigarette and wishing he hadn't quit smoking years ago. Maybe he could bum a smoke. He rises from the couch, smooths his skirt, and teeters in heels to the French doors of the veranda. A man leans against the rail, a large man looking larger with exaggerated shoulder pads. He turns and exposes an Arnold Schwarzenegger face. "Pardon me," Marilyn purrs. "Might you have a cigarette?"

"Unfortunately not," Arnold says in clipped Austrian. "But I could use one myself."

"What a perfect night for a Halloween party." Marilyn leans on the rail and sighs.

"Not quite perfect." Arnold eyes Marilyn in the dim light. "I see we are both huge Hollywood celebrities. Fame isn't all it's cracked up to be, right?"

"I couldn't live in this fantasy world," Marilyn says. "Fortunately it's almost midnight. We can toss these ridiculous masks."

Arnold looks at his watch. "Only minutes to go. You a friend of Elaine?"

"Actually I was hoping to be a friend of a friend of Elaine."

"Funny you said that." Arnold drops his accent. "I was hoping the same."

"But my expected friend didn't show."

"Neither did mine." He checks his watch again. "It's nearly midnight. We'd better return to the party for the unmasking." He holds the door and sees her in full light. He stops. She smiles.

He smiles. "Love that dimple on your chin."

LOST WAX

Caroline Harvey balances an English china tureen, her heels clacking on the kitchen tile floor, then fading on the dining room carpet. She lights candles, then fans two linen napkins and places them beside the plates. So beautiful. The violets on the china, the violet napkins, the violet candles. So beautiful. Mr. Harvey has an eye for beauty. He will appreciate this.

She sits at the table, spreads a napkin on her lap, and lifts a small cordial glass in a toast. Candlelight refracts and dances in the glass. "Isn't it beautiful?" she whispers.

She lifts the cover of the tureen and inhales a creamy mushroom potage, Mr. Harvey's favorite. She reaches across the table for his gold-rimmed bowl and ladles a small portion, then ladles her bowl. The grandfather clock in the foyer chimes six forty-five, fifteen minutes until Mr. Harvey's favorite program. She glances through lace-curtained windows, now dark in early November.

Light rain patters against the windows; unseasonal thunder growls long and low like a faraway freight train. She snugs the sweater that rests on her shoulders. Modest candlelight flickers, creating shadows that creep along the walls. The silence of the house disquiets her. Only the patter of rain and the *tick-tock, tick-tock* of the clock. She spoons the potage and lifts it to her lips. Shadows gesture like menacing arms, reaching, reaching for her. She dabs her lips with a napkin, then lifts the cordial glass and drains it.

Laurie stands at the door wearing her Larry's Fixit jacket, her hair bundled in a baseball cap, rain dripping off the roof. She shines her key chain flashlight on the doorbell plaque—*The Harveys*—then pushes the bell button and rehearses her introduction. *No, I'm not Larry. I'm Laurie. Larry is busy this time of year tuning furnaces. I get the light stuff. Like your Kenmore washer. Ha ha.*

THAT REMINDS ME

Laurie shuffles her tool bag and looks at the sky, a cold darkness smeared by gusts of rain. A school bus rounds the corner flashing gaudy red and yellow lights and stops behind her panel truck. A girl dismounts, shielding her head with a backpack.

"No one's home there," she yells when she spots Laurie.

Laurie waits. Larry had expected this to be a motor replacement. Likely a worn drive belt, Laurie thinks. Men tend to over-diagnose.

The curtain on the door's glass panel moves. "Yes?" comes a slight voice from within.

"I'm from Larry's Fixit. Here to fix your washer."

"You're not Larry."

"Right. I'm Laurie. But I'll fix your washer, Mrs. Harvey."

The door opens to a dark foyer. Candles glisten on the dining room table. A pungent aroma floats through the door. Garlic. Butter. Cream.

"I'm sorry. I didn't mean to interrupt your dinner," Laurie says, standing on the stoop.

"Come in. Come in. No interruption at all." Mrs. Harvey switches on a table lamp and eyes Laurie. Denim jacket and jeans, tool belt, lace-up boots. Corrugated soles, the type likely to retain caked dirt. She points to a rubber floor mat. "You can leave your shoes there. I didn't expect you this late."

A large black cat scoots out the door, startling Laurie. "Don't worry about him," Mrs. Harvey says. "He'll be back. If not tonight, tomorrow. Or the next day."

"My last call," Laurie says, scraping her boots on the mat. "I'll try to make it fast. And I'll need to keep my boots on. Running back and forth to the truck for tools, parts. I'll clean up my mess."

Mrs. Harvey purses her lips. "I suppose." Then she leads Laurie to the laundry room.

"How long has your machine been acting up?" Laurie pushes *wash* and listens for running water. Nothing. She kneels on the floor and removes the front panel.

"About a week," Mrs. Harvey says and reaches for a dust mop to gather balls of lint.

Laurie tugs at the drive belt. Taut. "Where's your circuit breaker box?"

Mrs. Harvey points to the wall. "Oh, my," she says when she

sees the red indicator. She turns an embarrassed face. "I'm sorry to have called you out for such a stupid mistake. Oh, my." She shields her face with both hands, then recovers. "If you haven't had dinner, please let me offer you a bowl of soup."

"If it tastes as good as it smells, you got yourself a deal."

Mrs. Harvey points to the bathroom. "You can wash in there."

"So you're Laurie of Larry's Fixit." Mrs. Harvey reaches for a bowl from the china cabinet and ladles the soup. "Are you and Larry married?"

"Seventeen years. Forever. And you, Mrs. Harvey. Am I sitting in Mr. Harvey's chair?"

"Perhaps, but it's not a problem."

"Beautiful china. Beautiful table. Special occasion?"

"Every occasion is special. You must know that, being married."

"Being married, I know every occasion is *not* special." Laurie spoons her soup, lifts it to her nose, and closes her eyes. "I'll give it an A for aroma." She tastes the soup and smacks her lips. "This is so good it has to be bad for you."

"As many good things are," Mrs. Harvey says. "Is Larry working tonight?"

"Probably 'til ten. Everybody waits 'til the last minute to have their furnace checked."

"You're certain he's checking furnaces?"

Laurie stops, her spoon halfway to her mouth. "What else would he be doing?"

"Don't get me started." Mrs. Harvey squints through once-kind eyes. "But since you ask . . . it's seven o'clock. You think your husband is on a service call. How can you be certain?"

"Because I know him, that's how." Laurie feels fatigue from a long day, chilled from damp hair and clothing, sorry she accepted the dinner invitation. She pictures being home snuggling on the couch, watching a program, waiting for Larry. And Larry will be there, she *is* certain, with a confidence she didn't know existed. Until now.

Mrs. Harvey stares at Laurie. "Marriage is a house of cards. One gust of ill wind and the whole thing collapses."

Laurie takes another spoonful of soup. "Was that your experience, Mrs. Harvey?"

Silence. Only the *tick-tock* of the clock, the patter of rain on the windows.

"So Mr. Harvey is *not* coming home," Laurie says. "You just set his place at the table. Hope springs eternal, right? How long has he been gone?"

Silence.

"Your dedication's commendable, Mrs. Harvey. Commendable and confusing. But it's your life."

Mrs. Harvey folds her napkin and places it on the table. "Please. Listen to me." Her eyes glisten in the candlelight. "I thought Mr. Harvey worked late too. Every night at the studio. He created custom jewelry, magnificent pieces for high society. Even royalty." She fingers an elaborate pendant on a gold neck chain and stares at the candles. "He sculpted intricate one-of-a-kind designs, then cast them using the lost wax process. His hair always smelled like hot wax.

"Then one night a friend saw him in the alley behind a bar. With another woman." She dabs her eyes with the napkin. "That was many years ago." She straightens in her chair, her chin high, her shoulders back. "But he'll be back. I'm certain of it."

Laurie tips her bowl for the last spoonful. "And so am I. You're a tough old gal, Mrs. Harvey." She pushes her chair back. "I'm on my way now. No charge for the service call. The soup was worth the price of the trip."

A cat meows at the door. "I'll walk you out, Laurie. And let Mr. Harvey in."

Caroline Harvey balances the china on a silver tray and carries it clattering to the kitchen. She flicks on the light and returns to the dining room to fold napkins and blow out candles. Tiny trails of black smoke rise from pools of aromatic hot wax.

She inhales. "So beautiful," she whispers. "So beautiful."

IRISES

Adele Prescott bends over her iris bed, clipping blooms that shriveled and died while she visited her sister in Denver. She remembers majestic blossoms that commandeered the garden, waving proud lavenders and apricots and whites, battling the vagaries of weather and the trampling of neighborhood dogs. Adele knows the feeling.

Alone with her flowers, she stands erect and removes a glove. She places a hand on the small of her back and stretches in late spring sun, high now, warm and blinding. If she is to enjoy widowhood, she must wear her straw.

As she stands, a car signals a turn into the drive. A squad car, low profile lights, gold lettering on the door.

Good Lord, Adele mouths. *Has someone been reading my mind?*

The car stops at the garage, and two officers alight. One, the driver, is stocky, with a confidant John Wayne stride, a holster clapping his hip, sewn pleats in his body-hugging shirt. Aviator sunglasses. The second, a miniature of the first, is younger, less threatening.

"Are you Mrs. Marshall Prescott?" The first officer doffs his hat and reveals a baldness that glistens in the sun.

She nods.

"I'm Sergeant Schoen, Washington County Sheriff Department. This is my partner Officer Nelson." He unbuttons his shirt pocket and retrieves a business card.

"Is he dead?"

"No, ma'am." The sheriff shakes his head. "No, ma'am. And I apologize if I startled you. Would you have him call this number please?"

"Yes," she says with slight relief. A pause, and then, "May I ask what this is about?"

"Just have him call me, if you would please." He cocks his head and wipes a handkerchief across his brow.

The card trembles in her hand. She sees her erect image in the lens of his glasses. *Strange,* she thinks. *Why am I not alarmed?*

He nods. "Good day, ma'am." They return to the car.

Something while I was gone? she wonders. The unidentified phone calls come to mind. The horror stories of men being shot for welshing on debts. The bank statement with ATM withdrawals from Mystic Lake. The early-to-work departures, the late-to-home arrivals.

"It's an addiction," the counselor had said. "He may have to hit bottom before he reforms. You may be able to help him." *Right,* she thought. *I can do that.*

The session had cost $140. For what? They had borrowed from her father, tapped into their IRA, applied for a second mortgage. She stares at the house. Georgian brick two-story with shuttered, small-paned windows. Hand-split shakes. Manicured lawn. Perennial flower gardens with cobblestone walks. A storybook setting.

She scans the garden with a desperate glance, breathing the musky odor of dead irises. Among the petal-less stems, one bloom remains, reaching for the sun. Its regal purple petals boast a mature beauty, a will to survive. Adele stoops to caress the bloom. A hummingbird buzzes her head and shocks her back to her clipping task.

She scans the perennial garden—the spent irises, the supple blades of lily leaves, the bursting peony buds. *How long will this be mine?* she wonders. *It could be gone in a year.* She must halt his profligate spending. If not, will there be enough to pay the hit man?

SEVENTEEN

"And this is the *Writers' Almanac* for Thursday, October second. It's the birthday of . . ."

October second. That's your birthday, Randy. How old would you be today? Seventeen. Seventeen years old today. Junior in high school. Football, maybe. Track.

You'd be seventeen. Weigh about 170, 175, I'd guess. Tended to favor your mother's side of the family. Big-boned. Heavy. Wonder if you could lift me and toss me in the air like I lifted you. Wonder if I could take you in wrestling. Probably not.

Seventeen. A girlfriend or two. Tended to favor me there. I can hear you.

"Dad, can I have the car tonight?"

"Sure. Be home by midnight."

"Ah, Dad."

"All right, one o'clock. No later."

Seventeen. Talking college. Breaking away. Walking out the door with all the confidence in the world. Leaving me to fret and worry while you're out practicing everything I taught you. Self-reliance. Be your own man. Be the architect of your fate.

You know those artists who draw pictures of missing kids showing how they'd look ten, fifteen years later? I've thought about that. I think I could guess. Coal black hair. A brush of mustache and sideburns. Square chin. Dark eyes squinting when you smile.

I'm less certain about how you'd think, how you'd act. Would you still have that independent streak? Would you lock up when you didn't get your way? Go stiff as a board if you didn't want to be held? Snuggle on my lap until you fell asleep at night? Well, not on my lap anymore.

Would you still munch dry Cheerios? Hate peas? Pick the chocolate chips out of cookies?

Would you have a dog like Mitzy that you crawled over and pulled her ears and tried to touch her eyes? You'd probably have a Lab that could swim and hunt and play football. Would you still hate cats after Buttons scratched you?

What would I be like? Still married to your mother, maybe. We couldn't deal with your . . . couldn't deal with your not being there.

But life goes on.

Or does it?

PROXY

A ten-minute drama with three female characters

Shirley Sanford follows Rosie the waitress to a table in a coffee shop.

ROSIE: What a lovely day, Mrs. Sanford. And I hear you have a wedding coming up in the family.

Shirley: Word gets around in a small town, doesn't it? Yes, my daughter Margie is getting married in June. The groom's mother, Joyce, is meeting me here today to plan the event.

ROSIE: Who's she marrying?

Shirley: Fred Compton. He's an investment banker. She was dating a carpenter, but his construction firm folded. What a shame.

ROSIE: Where's he from?

Shirley: You had to ask, didn't you? North Oaks.

ROSIE: Wow. High class. Neighbor of the Mondales, I expect. Or McKnights. Or Pillsburys.

    Bell rings.

Rosie: Oh, a customer. Maybe it's the groom's mom.

    Shirley pages through Modern Bride. *Rosie enters with Joyce.*

Shirley: Good morning, Joyce. How nice to see you. Please have a chair. What a lovely day, isn't it?

    Joyce sits, surveys the room, wipes bread crumbs from the table.

Joyce: Yes, it's a beautiful day.

ROSIE: You both want coffee?

Joyce: What kind of tea do you have?

ROSIE: Hot or iced.

Joyce: And your coffee? Starbucks? Caribou?

ROSIE: Nope. Folgers. On sale at Walmart this week.

Shirley: Anything to go with the coffee? Biscotti, maybe?

ROSIE: Ginger snap cookies.

Joyce: Just bring two coffees.

THAT REMINDS ME

Rosie writes ticket and exits.

Joyce: That's the problem with meeting on Monday. The club is closed. Well, we have lots of ground to cover. Flowers, music, menu, color scheme, invitation list, reception.

Shirley: I wish Margie was more interested in the planning. She said she'd be okay with a wedding at home, followed by a backyard barbecue. I understand they want to finance the wedding themselves.

Joyce: Yes. How noble. And how unrealistic. Now, starting with the invitation list . . .

Rosie enters with two cups of coffee.

ROSIE: How are the wedding plans coming? I love weddings, especially mine.

Joyce: Weddings? Plural? How many times have you been married? Two? Three?

ROSIE: Nope. Five. Goin' on six.

Joyce: Well, did you ever think that God intended you to be single?

ROSIE: Funny you should say that. That's exactly what my spiritual adviser said.

Joyce: You have a spiritual adviser?

ROSIE: Yup! My third husband, Charles. A born-again Christian. Took me on as a Junior Achievement project, I'd say. Tried for three months to get me to mend my ways. Finally, took his Bibles and Jim and Tammy Baker tapes and left.

Shirley: With all your expertise, Rosie, maybe you could help us with a few details. How about the reception menu?

ROSIE: My favorite reception was after my second wedding. To Walt. My mother planned the menu, but she didn't know Walt's people. They all showed up with hot dishes, plates of bars, celery stalks stuffed with peanut butter, Jell-O salad with fruit cocktail. Walt's mother just moved the food around to make room. She cleared a tray of triangle sandwiches and replaced it with a platter of pigs-in-a-blanket. Folks loved it.

Joyce: So much for the menu. What about music? The acoustics are great at the Club. I was thinking about a string quartet.

Shirley: Margie has friends who have a band.

ROSIE: My fourth wedding. To Raymond. Or was he third? Anyway, Ray and his friends loved to sing, so we had a karaoke machine. Ray was a cowboy, and the wedding had a western theme. I wore a fringed, white leather vest and white Levis. White cowboy boots. They even got me up there on stage. I sang "These Boots Are Made for Walking."

Joyce: You wore white at your *fourth* wedding?

ROSIE: Sure. I already had the vest, and the boots were on sale. Easy choice.

Joyce: I'm not sure that's helpful. Let's talk about attendants. Relatives or friends? Three? Four? Five? Fred will want his three brothers.

Shirley: And Margie will want her sisters to be maid of honor and first bridesmaid. We'll need one more.

ROSIE: Don't overdo the family thing is my advice. At my last wedding, to Brad, we pulled a couple pedestrians off the street into the JP's office. They were happy to do it. Saved someone buying dresses and renting tuxes, and saved us from buying gifts. We went to the bar after the ceremony, and they even bought us a couple drinks.

Joyce: Rosie, I know you're trying to be helpful, but we're not making any progress.

Shirley: You have to admit she's given us something to think about. I never was certain they should marry in the first place. And a big wedding would add mockery to a short marriage.

Joyce: I'm glad you said that, Shirley. I've had misgivings myself. Maybe they should just . . . just live together for a while. Test the waters, so to speak. *Pause.* I wonder if I can return my dress.

Shirley: You already bought a dress? What color?

Joyce: Beige. Ann Landers says the mother of the groom should shut up and wear beige.

ROSIE: Well now, that was easy, wasn't it? I'll get the check.

KINDNESS

The first sip of a full-bodied Cabernet Sauvignon reminds me of Bette—of the day she walked out of my life. As the wine touched my lips, I remember she announced she was leaving. The taste and the announcement surprised me, jolted me. As the wine swirled around my tongue, she grabbed her car keys. The savory dark fruit flavor and my new freedom created baffling delight. As wine guzzled down my throat, she walked out the door. The result was an unexpected aftertaste, a perplexing sweetness.

Bette's timing was impeccable. She had seized the moment to move in while I suffered self-diagnosed depression from the breakup of an earlier affair. For a couple months, we relived the Cold War, her smoking in the bedroom, blasting the walls with the Red Hot Chili Peppers, stashing half-empty beer bottles in the sink. We always knew our relationship was a gamble. I didn't have the balls to call it quits. She did.

Mystery was what Bette was all about, and at first I found it intriguing. But mystery in a relationship only goes so far. Without feedback, a man wonders about his competence, doubts his prowess. When I asked her why she never said she liked me, let alone loved me —her answer: a woman needs to keep a man guessing. *Wrong.* When I asked her why she never had an orgasm, she claimed she did. All the time. I told her I wouldn't have known. She twirled a strand of my hair around her finger and smiled her trademark twisted smile. "A woman must project an aura of mystery." *Wrong again.*

A guy friend who counsels grieving families assumed I required loss therapy and walked me through the stages of grief, all five or six of them. He cautioned me to move slowly, to be honest with myself, to own my sorrow, my regrets. Funny, I had no regrets. At our final session over coffee, my counselor friend urged me to remember the good times. "If I were to ask you the highlight of your relationship with

Bette, what would it be?"

I didn't hesitate. "The moment she walked out the door."

As I sip a glass of wine at the keyboard, I notice hints of Bette in my rough drafts—her infectious laughter, her lithe body seated in a lotus position, her holding my gaze when we argued. But I don't miss Bette. I don't miss her at all. The tropical fish miss her more than I do. Half of them died. Not from broken hearts but from lack of feeding.

When Bette left, I resumed my bad habit of joining the guys for Happy Hour at the Broken Hart. Last night I greeted the gang and sat at my assigned corner stool hand-warming private stock Cab in a stemware glass. The room was air-conditioned cold, a slick wet feeling on the bar. My motley pals chugged beer from sweaty bottles or swilled mixed drinks from plastic glasses.

The air was heavy with raucous laughter. On the jukebox, Willy Nelson wailed his lament that you were always on my mind, reminding me for a moment of Bette. A NASCAR race, muted on the television, flashed a brilliant kaleidoscope of reds and blues and oranges. A State Fair aroma of fried hamburgers and onions wafted from the grill. A textbook male environment. I wanted to hug the world with my odd but wondrous feeling of well-being. Like the first sip of a pricey Cab.

Two women entered the bar, and conversations stopped while the guys checked them out. The women acted impervious to the attention and headed for bar stools at a right angle to me, no sign of a break in their chatter and laughter. One younger, one older. Friends, not relatives. Swimsuits under neon sarongs, visored caps, sun-reddened arms and throat.

"Canoeing?" I asked.

"For three days," the younger one said, "and it rained all three nights." The older woman tilted away and buried her face in a menu.

"This your destination?"

The older woman threw an icy glance and returned to the menu. "Finally," the younger one said. "We're camping north of town, and we have a problem. We can't find dry wood for our campfire tonight. Everything is soaked."

"Did you walk here from the campsite?"

"No, we drove from the Twin Cities in two vehicles, one parked at our point of entry and one at our campsite here."

"I can help you with the firewood," I said. "Which one is your vehicle?"

"The pickup with the kayaks in back," the younger one said.

The older one managed a smile.

I finished my Cab and, surrendering to my wondrous feeling of well-being, scrounged a couple armloads of wood from a neighbor's shed and loaded it in the truck. Back in the bar, I waved a slab of dry cedar. "In my town, you don't have problems."

The younger one rose from her stool. The older one extended her hand.

"Come back again some time." I waved them back and walked out the door.

The following afternoon, I half-expected to see the two women at the bar. I fantasized that, after a night of rum and Cokes around a blazing campfire, they exhausted strategies on how to demonstrate gratitude for the dry aromatic firewood. How they speculated about the mysterious gentleman, dissected his motivation, and concluded as the last drop of rum kissed their lips, it was a random act of kindness. But one to be rewarded.

The truck with protruding kayaks wasn't parked in front of the Broken Hart. Instead, a horde of heavily chromed Harleys parked in precise orientation gleamed in the parking area like an ad for Armor All. Inside, my gang sat at their assigned stools. An overweight 612-er in plaid Bermudas and knee socks sat at my corner. I slapped a few comrades on the back and said *Hi* to the barmaid.

"I have a message for you," she said and handed me a glass of Cab and a note written on a guest check.

I struggled with the handwriting. Something like, *You left before we could offer our thanx. We hear you're a writer. Can't wait to buy your books.*

So you don't have to wait and die to collect your rewards in heaven. I stuffed the note in my pocket and paid for my Cab.

The fry cook yelled *Order up* and plunked two baskets of onion rings on the counter. The barmaid hustled them to a table in the far corner.

"A woman was asking for you earlier," one of the guys said. "Wanted to know if we expected you tonight."

"Woman or women? I may know who they are."

"Woman. I think that's her sitting at the back table with the bikers. She's looking at you. Smiling."

You know the feeling when your gut says don't look, when your years of accumulated intuition say get the hell out, but your mother's tirades against rudeness and your own curiosity prevail? I turned and faced a smiling, onion ring-waving Bette. A wind-blown, now blond Bette. A couple sizes larger, obvious even as she sat, wearing a scoop-necked T-shirt inscribed *Kinky Sex is…* I couldn't read the rest.

I waved to her and let Mom's rules of conduct propel me to the table. Bette sat with a group of leather-vested bikers, red handkerchiefs tied around their heads, bushel-sized beards. Two pitchers of tap beer sweated on the table. "Pull up a chair, stranger," Bette said holding a bottle of Blue Moon, and slid over to make room for me.

"What brings you to our fair city?" I extended my hand for her to shake. Six males and one other female sat at the table. I slid into a chair between Bette and a burly biker.

"Doc," Bette said to the biker. "This is my author friend."

"Hi, author friend. Shandra has told us about you."

I turned to Bette. "You changed your name?"

"Had to," Bette whispered. "When I put on the extra pounds, they called me Bette the Butt."

"What are you writing now?" Doc asked. Despite the beard and leather, he appeared well-groomed. His speech hinted at elocution classes. East coast. Maybe Ivy League.

"Another collection of short stories," I said. It sounded apologetic. Doc smiled and drained his glass.

I picked up snippets of conversation from others at the table—the demise of entrepreneurship, the global rise of nationalism, the reshaping of American politics—and turned to Bette, now Shandra. "Who are these people?"

"Doc, tell my friend about your group."

"Happy to do so." Doc refilled his glass. "We call ourselves the Writer Riders. We love Harleys and we love writing. Everyone here is published, some of us many times." He grinned and punched my arm. "And not just short stories."

"Sweet," I said, "but how does she fit into this?"

"We also mentor kids," Doc said, "trying to make the world a better place with little acts of kindness. Shandra works at Social Services and recommends prospective students. And she likes to ride."

Bette pushed her chair back. "Come outside with me while I have a cigarette." She pulled a box of American Spirits from her fanny pack. "We have to talk."

Run, my survivor-self yelled. My mannered-self said, "Excuse us for a couple minutes, Doc." I followed her past the bar stools amid a chorus of throat clearings, could have followed the trail of her signature fragrance Chloe blindfolded.

"I know you love coincidence." Bette lit a cigarette. "I couldn't help but notice a tad of it in your latest book."

The late afternoon sun played peekaboo through a copse of trees and reflected in her eyes. Brown eyes looking even browner on a blonde. The extra pounds had settled in the right places and gave her a wholesome appearance. A warm red windburn on her face had replaced her wan never-outside look. I felt unsettled. I needed a Cab.

"Funny coincidence isn't it, that your protagonist's name is Beth." She pointed to herself. "Bette. Funny that Beth drinks Blue Moon beer. Funny that Beth smokes American Spirits." She blew a mouthful of smoke at me.

"You're flattering yourself," I said in self-defense. "Beth is the gal next door. Born and raised in rural Minnesota. Maybe wants to dedicate her life to a church-sponsored nonprofit. Wants to experience life on the other end of the spectrum to know herself, know if that other world appeals to her."

As my defense accelerated, my confidence grew. "Hence the drinking, the smoking, the rock concerts. The approach to the bedroom door but never into the bed. Not Beth." I held Bette's stare. "Not until she meets Mr. Wonderful whom she marries, if you read that far."

Bette snuffed her cigarette. "My boyfriend extracted a promise from me to threaten you with legal action for invasion of privacy. He thought ten thou would settle the issue."

I laughed.

"Short of that, my boyfriend said I should get ten percent of the royalties."

"What's ten percent of nothing?"

"All right, all right. I did what I had to do." She managed her trademark twisted smile. "Something else. In my haste to leave you, I forgot a few things."

Right, I thought. *Her collection of ceramic frogs, the exercise bicycle, her half of the rent.*

"I forgot to thank you."

THAT REMINDS ME

I saw tears forming.

"Thank you for tolerating my childish behavior, for sheltering me in my moment of need."

"Oh, come on," I said. "You can do better than that."

"This isn't easy." She reached for my hand. "Listen to me. I want to thank you for all your kindness. I didn't appreciate it until it was gone."

"Expression of gratitude noted," I said, and reached for her other hand.

"One more thing." She pulled her hands away and her brown eyes teared. "I forgot to say goodbye."

She smiled her twisted smile.

"So, goodbye."

YOUR HEART'S DESIRE

Julia Roberts leaned back in the lilac leather chair, crossed her legs, and dangled a strapped pump from her painted toes. She raised her fingers to her chin in a prayer position and smiled her global warming smile.

"This is your final question on *Your Heart's Desire*, the Celebrity Quiz Show," the announcer said. "If you answer correctly, you win anything your heart desires. Miss Roberts, are you ready?"

Julia swept the audience with a slow glance of chocolate brown eyes and nodded to the announcer. "I'm ready."

The announcer sat upright, raised his glasses on his nose, and cleared his throat. The audience sat still, spellbound. "Name five American winners of the Nobel Peace Prize."

Julia leaned forward and flashed a knowing smile. She held the audience in a suspenseful, dramatic pause. "Theodore Roosevelt, Woodrow Wilson, the American Red Cross, and Jimmy Carter," she answered. "And Martin Luther King."

The audience erupted. The announcer double-checked the answer list. Julia leaned back and smiled.

"Correct," screamed the announcer. "You've won *Your Heart's Desire*. And Julia Roberts, what is your heart's desire?"

Julia paused again, playing with the audience and the announcer. Her lips parted in a smile that rivaled the Grand Canyon. "I want to spend a weekend on Maui with Jerry . . . something, the author of *Good Shepherd*."

The silence in the auditorium was deafening. The announcer cocked his head in a quizzical pose. Julia smiled.

When I returned to the house after chores, the incoming call light on the telephone blinked. Fourteen calls. I washed garden dirt from my hands, rinsed mosquito spray from my face, and brushed hay chaff from my hair. The telephone rang.

"Have you been watching television?" an unidentified voice asked.

"No," I answered. "I don't watch television. I don't own a television. Who is this?"

"Well, if you don't watch television, what do you do?"

"Get to the point," I said. "Another World Trade Center bombing? Another pandemic? Another assassination?"

"Nope. Better than that."

The phone call came the next morning from the publicist of *Your Heart's Desire*. Had I heard of the show? *Yes.* Was I familiar with the format? *Yes, vaguely.* Had I heard the results of the Julia Roberts episode? *Yes, from neighbors, friends, family, co-workers, high school classmates, total strangers.* Was I available the week of September 15 for a trip to Maui? I hesitated. "Let me check my calendar." I placed the phone on the counter for a respectable interval. "I think I can make that work."

We met at the Premier Club at Maui's Kahului Airport. She sat by the window beside a bouquet of orchids. The tails of her white blouse were tied in a casual knot, revealing a buttery tanned stomach. Her hair fell like fresh cut clover across her shoulders. She wore small oval glasses and smiled as she read my book *Good Shepherd*.

"Julia," I said, steadying myself against a lamp table.

"Jerry," she said. She stood, almost to my height and smiled. The room lit up like it had been struck by lightning.

We rode to the Grand Wailea in her limo, talking about the book. *What prompted it? Were the characters real? Who owned the rights?*

"I'm flattered by your interest," I said, "but what are you leading up to?"

"I'd like to try my hand at directing," she said, "and direct a movie based on your book. I want to play a role too, maybe have you create a character for me."

I pursed my lips and stared at swaying palm trees, hedges of indulgent hibiscus, orchids profuse as dandelions. "I think I could do that."

"And I'd like Bob Duval to play one of the Good Shepherd residents. Might have to flesh out his character, but I'll bet you could do that too."

That moment I could rewrite *Gone with the Wind.* "I have a few short stories inspired by those characters," I said.

"Great." She grinned. "We'll talk about that."

We checked into the hotel, she conquering the lobby with a long-legged stride and a smile behind rose-colored sun glasses. I followed, feeling very Minnesotan in my Hawaiian shirt, white painter pants, and Jesus sandals.

"Meet me at the gate to the beach at nine," she said.

I strolled the hotel grounds—sparkling pools, a half-mile river, a waterfall, tropical gardens, ambrosial plumerias, back to the lobby the size of my hometown.

Eons later, nine o'clock arrived. Eyes closed, I stood before a full-length mirror—new swim trunks, beach towel thrown casually over a shoulder, twirling un-needed sunglasses. Bougainvillea and birds of paradise scented the lanai. Guitars strummed from behind stuccoed garden walls. Coconut oil and lime juice and fresh grated ginger flavored the sea air.

I looked in the mirror. God. My body was as white as a hospital patient's. My skinny legs belonged to a stork. My hair was frizzy from humidity. I guzzled a glass of Merlot. Then another. "What am I worried about?" I said to my fortified self. "She was married to Lyle Lovett."

We met at the beach and talked until midnight about her movies, the twins, her ranch in Taos, her directorial debut. She asked about my life, where I had been and where I was going. The hours flew.

The moon peeked over the horizon, and waves of the wide Pacific lapping on the shore fractured the moon's reflection. We shared a bottle of Merlot. Guitars strummed in the distance.

"Wanna play From Here to Eternity?" I asked.

Julia laughed. The moon reflected off a perfect set of gleaming teeth. "What's that?"

"Did you see the movie? Deborah Kerr and Burt Lancaster in the beach scene? Right here on the islands."

"Refresh my memory," she said.

I leaned on one elbow in the sand. "The moon is shining," I said in a low sexy register. "Deborah and Burt are lying on the beach. They kiss, and the waves wash up the shore and douse them. Deborah shivers, and we don't know if it's the cold water or the hot kiss."

"Wait a minute." She smiled. "Didn't we agree this would be a business relationship?"

I gritted my teeth. "Agreed, but I don't do platonic very well." I traced her smile with my fingers, a journey that took minutes. She closed her eyes. I kissed her with a gentleness that surprised me.

She leaned back and stared at the rolling surf. Flecks of moonlight danced in her eyes. A trace of mischief tickled her smile. She lifted the Merlot and drained the final drops, then relaxed on the beach towel. "You're from Minnesota, right?

I nodded.

"Well, that's a first." She reached for my arms. "All right," she teased. "Let's see where it takes us. To the book. To the movie. Or to your heart's desire."

ACKNOWLEDGMENTS

Grateful acknowledgment is made to the following newspapers and journals for the previous publication of these poems and stories:

Talking Stick Volume 11, 2002
"Sawyer"

Talking Stick Volume 13, 2004
"Sixth Sense"

Talking Stick Volume 14, 2005
"Cat Tale" (previously published as "Monologue")

Talking Stick Volume 15, 2006
"Jed Mueller's Auction" (previously published as
       "Mueller's Auction")

Talking Stick Volume 16, 2007
"Blue Mason Jar"
"Theme and Variations"

Talking Stick Volume 17, 2008
"Ice Out"
"Single Space"

Talking Stick Volume 18, 2009
"Bridges" (previously published as "Redemption")

Talking Stick Volume 19, 2010
"Weather"

Talking Stick Volume 21, 2012
"And a Bier for Dad"
"Man of the Year"

Talking Stick Volume 22, 2013
"Little Women"

Talking Stick Volume 24, 2015
"Love. Birth. Death."
"Witness"

Talking Stick Volume 25, 2016
"Your Heart's Desire"

Sebeka-Menahga Review Messenger
"In Memoriam: President Gerald R. Ford"
"Legend of the Skull"
"State of the Union"
"Reflections on the Water"

Made in the USA
Charleston, SC
18 August 2016